Non-Fiction
739.27 Sp8

Sprintzen, Alice
Jewelry : basic techniques a

9000602710

DO NOT REMOVE CARD FROM POCKET

Mead Public Library
Sheboygan, Wisconsin

Each borrower is held responsible for all library
materials drawn on his card and for all fines
accruing on same.

DEMCO

Jewelry

Basic Techniques and Design

Jewelry

Basic Techniques and Design

ALICE SPRINTZEN

Chilton Book Company
Radnor, Pennsylvania

Copyright © 1980 by Alice Sprintzen
All Rights Reserved
Published in Radnor, Pennsylvania by Chilton Book Company
and simultaneously in Don Mills, Ontario, Canada,
by Nelson Canada Limited
Library of Congress Catalog Card No. 80-958
ISBN 0-8019-6828-3 *hardcover*
ISBN 0-8019-6830-5 *paperback*
Manufactured in the United States of America
Designed by Arlene Putterman

Front cover: Mary Lee Hu. Choker of fine and sterling
silver, lacquered copper. 1978.
Back cover: Bob Natalini. Pendant of polyester, silver,
tropical beetle, functioning electronic parts. 1977.
Barbara Mail. "The Orchid and the White Whale." Pin/
container of ivory, 14K colored golds, silver, lens,
dried orchid, pink tourmaline.

2 3 4 5 6 7 8 9 0   9 8 7 6 5 4 3 2 1

739.27
Sp8
c.1

602710

To David
and Daniel,
with love and appreciation

789.29
528
v. 1

Contents

Acknowledgments

I would like to express my gratitude to the following people and organizations for their generous sharing of expertise and time: Chuck Evans, Tom Farrell, Dorothy Lavine, Michael McCann, Barbara Mail, Bob Natalini, Renee O'Brien, Rae Raff, Carol Steen, American Crafts Council, the World Craft Council, and Richard Winter of CLM Photo.

The following companies generously contributed photographs and/or information: Allcraft Tool and Supply Company, Kerr Manufacturing Company, Polyproducts Corporation, and William Dixon Company.

I am particularly grateful to Elyse Sommer, without whose encouragement this book would not have been possible.

Special thanks go to Shirley Hochman for her continued support and assistance.

Finally, an expression of appreciation to Bernice Ballen for all that she has given.

Preface

This book presents information to guide and inspire the jeweler in finding his or her own path. There is no one correct way to make jewelry. Rather there are techniques and approaches that jewelers have arrived at after much experimentation, and these methods may help others find their way. I have emphasized that creation is an outgrowth of the individual's experience. Statements by artists about their work are included throughout the text in order to show how others view their journey. One should keep in mind that it is difficult, if not impossible, to put this experience into words.

A series of projects teach skills and the use of tools, building from simple to more advanced processes. The novice would do best to start the book at the beginning, using it as a step-by-step text. Thus a foundation is built from which the jeweler can begin combining techniques and using them in unique ways. Although each project utilizes skills and tools used in previous projects, the jeweler with prior experience can delve in at any point and use the book as a reference, or use it to learn a specific technique.

Tools and materials are introduced as they are used in the projects. Their use is explained the first time they are mentioned. The beginner may use the index to refer to previous projects if there is any question about the use of a tool or material. Where possible, substitute materials and tools are suggested in the interest of saving the jeweler the expense and time necessary to purchase specialized tools when experimenting in each technique.

The text is written simply and the instructions are detailed so they can be followed with ease. Photographs and diagrams make the processes clear. Suggestions are given with each project to serve as a guide for taking the process further.

Design is emphasized throughout the book. As you develop technical skills, options for design expand. Examples of artists' work have been selected not only to illustrate techniques but because each piece makes a strong and unique statement.

Two often-neglected aspects of the jeweler's craft are the hazards that are met in the workshop and the creative possibilities for display of the finished work. I have devoted a chapter to each of these topics.

Most projects requiring metal may be executed in copper, brass, bronze, and nickel silver as well as in gold and silver, the more precious metals. Use of the less expensive metals will yield excellent results. These metals can be purchased at most jewelry supply stores. Each metal exhibits unique qualities. The chapter on combining metals will show how small amounts of precious metals can be used to add the elements of color and preciousness to a larger piece, without requiring great expense.

The chapter on creating jewelry from materials other than metal presents a background for working in materials such as wood, plastic, found objects, clay and fabric.

Jewelry making is a merging of expression, technique, and function. The primary emphasis is on the handwrought object, not on mass production. It is the process as well as the product which makes the craft meaningful. Learning the technique is satisfying in itself—the satisfaction of a job well done.

Jewelry

Basic Techniques and Design

Designing Jewelry

1

Creative Resources

It is in our nature as humans to be creative. There lies a challenge to free our imagination and see the world in new ways. Developing the ability to value our intuitions, to stay with an idea until it feels "right," and to be appreciative of our inner sources of design widens our range of experience and adds new dimension to our lives. This is not to say that we cannot learn from the teachings of others. Another's point of view and knowledge may add to our creative resources.

Just about anything that we perceive or experience can inspire a piece of jewelry. Every experience changes us to some extent and adds to the perspective from which we see things. We come into contact with nature's creations and see how she is guided by function. Often, however, we take for granted and do not truly observe what beauty there is around us. If we try now to draw a fly, for example, we will see how little we know of the commonplace. What are its colors, lines, textures, shapes, proportions, and movements? There is an inexhaustible number of perspectives from which we may view anything.

Other artists and their creations are another source of inspiration for the jeweler. A visit to a gallery, museum, library, or artist's studio may bring us in contact with a different angle of vision. Viewing another's work is a visual means of communication from which one can articulate a new creation. We need not limit ourselves to studying the work of other jewelers, however. Inspiration may be gained from painters, commercial designers, photographers, architects, and, in particular, sculptors, for jewelry is sculpture in miniature.

FIG. 1–1   Nature as a source of design. *Drawing by Rae Raff.*

The germ of an idea may also grow from poetry, prose, music, dance, and drama. They, too, speak a language that may touch off something within us. Dreams and emotions are also a rich source of inspiration. Some artists keep a sketchbook handy. Ideas that surface spontaneously can be recorded and translated into tangible form before they are lost.

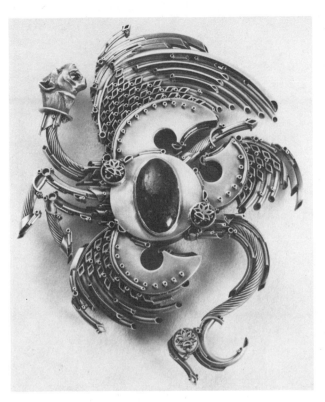

FIG. 1–2　Richard Mawdsley. "Angle of the Altai." Pin of sterling silver and lapis lazuli, fabricated with cast head. *Courtesy of the artist.*

The materials and processes used in jewelry making are themselves suggestive of designs. Qualities such as shape, texture, color, maleability, and even decay may be exploited if time is taken to observe what is already there. Consider the method of the prehistoric artist who searched the rock for the form of an animal and then proceeded to develop the forms suggested by the rock. Allowing the material itself to speak may carry us in interesting directions. Materials discarded from previous works may have an "afterlife," and they may provide the germ of an idea for a new work.

THE ARTIST SPEAKS: RICHARD HELZER

Each piece of my work is based on a system. The system I use is sometimes a mathematical formulation that usually creates a pattern. Sometimes I use a system of dimensional relationships which create a formal theme that is used throughout the piece.

Probably the most important visual aspect I use in my work is the combination of acrylics with gold, bronze, and sterling silver. The acrylic material gives me color and a linear movement which is important to the overall effect I am trying to achieve. I consider myself a "formalist" in that I have a very orderly approach to the development of each idea. I like to work with hard-edged geometric

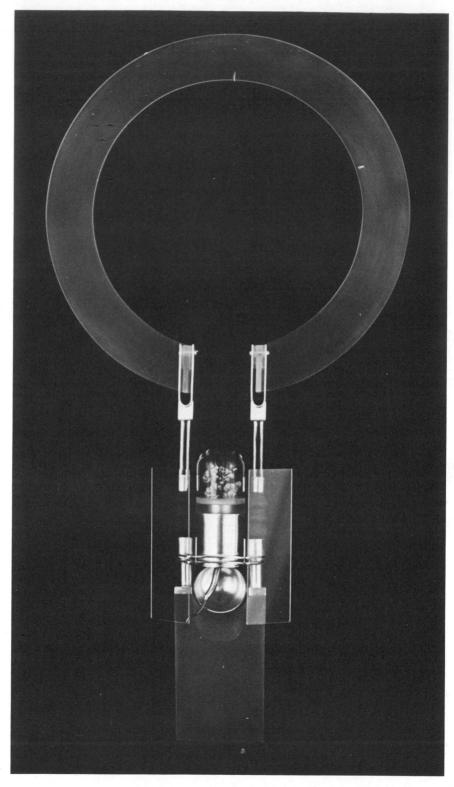

FIG. 1–3   Kelly Morris. "Outgrowth." Neckpiece of Plexiglas, glass, rubber, fabricated brass, copper, and sterling silver with copper electroforming. *Courtesy of the artist.*

shapes, such as a triangle or parallelogram, combined with a machinelike image. My interest in these shapes is a result of living and working in a modern, technological society surrounded by machines.

THE ARTIST SPEAKS: DOROTHY LAVINE

I want to be personal, magical, human. My jewelry stems from the excitement that occurs when I see an object or the relationship between objects or the way something moves—that makes me want to capture that response in permanent form. I keep working until the jewel has a life of its own, until it becomes the object that embodies the feelings that I originally experienced.

THE ARTIST SPEAKS: JACLYN DAVIDSON

Throughout my investigation of precious-metal work, "statement" has been the most important consideration for me. The images in my work deal with human beings and their environment. I find it fascinating to observe the self-conscious movements, the verbal foi-

FIG. 1–4   David Poston. Necklace, bracelet, and ring of forged stainless steel. 1978. *Photo by the artist.*

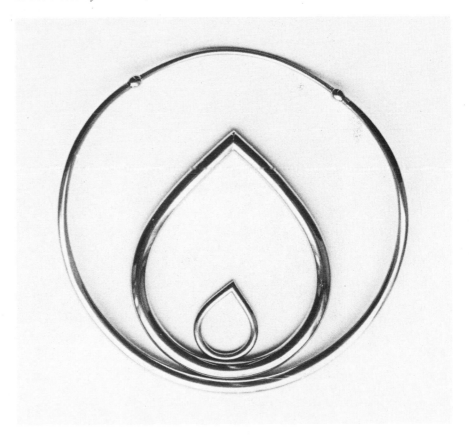

bles, and the complicated patterns of social behavior that define 20th-century Western man. As pieces begin to form from the seemingly undirected surfacing of these observations, I do not ask why of the developing relationships, only why not. My goal, for example, in designing a bracelet is to "get around the wrist" with a totally wearable flow of concepts. It is not mere enhancement of the body that I work toward, but rather, "what manner of cerebral message can I give you to wear?"

Design and Function

Whatever your source of design may be, and I have mentioned only a few, it is important to design jewelry with function in mind. Because jewelry is made to be worn, comfort and durability should be of vital concern to the jeweler. Consideration should also be given to the personality, taste, and physical characteristics of the wearer.

The following are some functional design considerations:
- Weight of earrings
- Vulnerability of a ring or a belt buckle
- Flexibility of an anklet
- Ease in opening a clasp
- Protrusions on a piece of jewelry that could get caught on clothing
- Relative size of a piece in relation to the size of the wearer
- The circumstances under which the piece will be worn

THE ARTIST SPEAKS: ARLINE FISCH

The current interest in "body sculpture," "body jewelry," and "sculpture to wear" reflects my concern with an increase in the scale and importance of personal adornments, but the terminology makes me uneasy because I worry about the place of the person. A person is more than a body or a moving pedestal for a piece of sculpture. A person has character and mood and style, which mark his or her identity as an individual apart from all other individuals. This aspect of a human being desires and determines ornamentation almost more than the body itself.

My interest is in large-scale jewelry that ornaments and enhances both the human form and the personality in ways that are exciting and dramatic, yet personal and wearable.

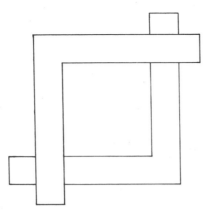

FIG. 1–5   Adjustable L frame for cropping a design.

Developing an Idea

One excellent method of developing an idea is to trace sections you like of a design and to redesign less pleasing parts. Numerous variations may be made from the original design, or you may wish to proceed from the redrawn design. Make successive sketches until you arrive at the best solution.

A frame may be used to zoom in on a selected section of the sketch. As a photographer looks through a camera and chooses a small portion of the whole, so this method aids in searching a complex sketch for its most satisfying parts. To make a frame, cut two identical L shapes out of paper. These shapes will overlap, forming rectangular frames of adjustable sizes to help you scan the sketch and crop sections that are most successful (figure 1–5).

Another simple approach is to cut out two-dimensional shapes from construction paper and arrange them in various ways until you come upon a pleasing design.

Because jewelry is three dimensional, many people prefer to work with a model to explore design possibilities. Thick paper or 26-gauge aluminum may be used to make the model. Paper may be drawn over the edge of either a table or scissors in order to achieve a curved form. It can be cut, twisted, pierced, folded, fringed, stapled, and glued with rubber cement. If a metallic look is preferred, the final paper model may be sprayed or brushed with metallic paint.

Some jewelers prefer to work directly, without making preliminary sketches. If you choose this spontaneous approach, you must be willing to discard or recycle pieces that are not successful. Direct experimentation should not be seen as wasteful, but rather as an important stage in developing your creation. Scrap metal may be resold or used in casting, or it may find new life in a future work.

People who have never designed before are sometimes overwhelmed by the limitless possibilities before them. In order to build some confidence and find a starting place, develop designs from doodles, children's drawings, photos, or other sources. Even working with a number such as your birthdate or zip code may provide a place to begin and also yield surprisingly interesting results.

Some artists choose a theme and develop it in a number of pieces until they feel that they have exhausted all fruitful possibilities.

Basic Techniques

2

In this chapter, instructions are given for making a pierced pendant, a simple soldered bracelet, and a belt buckle. In making these projects, you will learn the important techniques of piercing, sawing, polishing (by hand and machine), and soldering. These techniques are basic to most jewelry making in metal.

DESIGNING YOUR WORK: POSITIVE AND NEGATIVE SPACE

A simple pierced pendant is shown in figure 2–1. In piercing, pieces are removed from the sheet metal, and the "holes" become a major element of the design. Thus, in designing any pierced work, you must consider both positive and negative shapes. The metal that is removed is the negative shape. The remaining form is the positive shape.

As you make a design for your pendant, think as carefully about the negative shapes as the positive. Develop the ability to make positive and negative shapes interchangeable by training your eye to bring the negative forward and allowing the positive to recede. For example, when you cut a circle from a sheet of metal, you should see not only a rectangle with a hole in it but also a circle on a rectangular background. If you look at your fingers spread in front of you, you will see your hand as the positive shape. However, you can reverse the image so that the spaces between your fingers become the positive space, the dominant design element. In training your eye, it is sometimes helpful to turn a piece sideways or upside down to break habitual ways of seeing.

FIG. 2–1   Pendant made by piercing and sawing.

The pin in figure 2–2 is a more complex application of piercing, and it may suggest some ideas for your own work. But keep your first few designs simple.

Sawing and Piercing: Making a Pendant

Materials.   Your design for the pendant, 18-gauge sheet metal, jeweler's saw, saw blades of various sizes, beeswax or a bar of soap, center punch, hand drill or swivel-head pin vise and various size bits, steel surface plate, V-board and clamp, bench pin, files, needle files, emery paper (240, 320, 400, 600 grits), crocus cloth, sanding stick, tripoli, rouge, two polishing sticks, two pairs of flat or chain-nose pliers, jump rings, chain.

Transferring the Design to Metal

After drawing your design on a sheet of paper, glue the design onto the metal so that the metal is used economically. Use a water-soluble glue or rubber cement. If rubber cement is used, coat both surfaces to be joined and allow them to dry for a few minutes before putting them together.

Two other methods of transferring your design are to draw in pencil directly on the metal or to place carbon paper or white transfer paper between the design and the metal and draw over the design. In either case, it is advisable to go over your lines on the metal with a sharp scribe, lightly scratching the surface.

Piercing Holes

To pierce small circles in metal, use a hand drill and twist drills (bits) of various sizes (figure 2–3). To start the hole, first tap a center punch or nail into the area to be cut out. (When using the punch, work on the steel surface plate to prevent the metal from becoming excessively distorted. See figure 2–34, which shows a surface plate.) The resulting depression will prevent the pin vise from jumping around while the hole is being drilled (figure 2–4).

Larger circles may be punched out with a metal disc cutter (figure 2–5). To use the disc cutter, insert the sheet metal into the slot under the desired size hole. Using a heavy hammer, strike the corresponding punch, sharp edge down, through the hole. Sometimes several blows are necessary to pierce the metal completely. Never hit the sharp end of the punch with a hammer, for that will dull the cutting edge. A wood, rawhide, or plastic mallet can be used to help remove the punch from a tight hole.

The Jeweler's Saw

Although metal shears may be used to cut large shapes from thin metal, cutting thicker metal or intricate shapes requires a jeweler's

FIG. 2–2   Pat Garrett. "Riding Into the Sunset." Pierced pin of sterling silver, 14K gold, Morrison Ranch jasper, and Mexican fire opal. 1978. *Courtesy of the artist.*

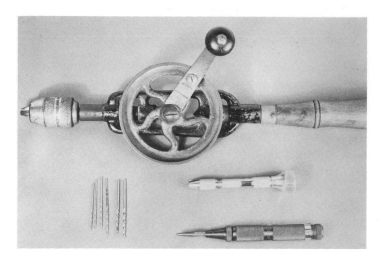

FIG. 2–3 Drilling tools. Clockwise from top: Hand drill (brace), pin vise, automatic center punch, twist drills (bits).

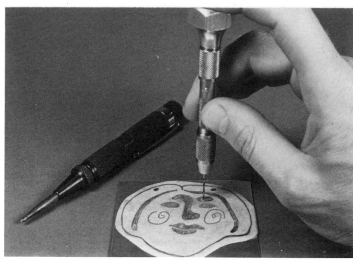

FIG. 2–4 Drill holes in each of the shapes to be sawed out after using the center punch to start the hole.

saw. If you have never used a jeweler's saw, it is a good idea to experiment on scrap materials before working on a piece of jewelry. To get acquainted with the saw, try cutting curved and straight lines using thin and thick blades. Cut shapes from the edge of a metal sheet and from the middle.

Removing internal sections of the design before sawing the outer edge will help maintain maximum support while sawing. In order to cut out shapes from the middle of a metal sheet, drill holes to accommodate the sawblade.

Loading and Using the Saw

To load the saw frame, place the blade with the teeth facing outward, away from the saw frame and pointing toward the handle. To achieve the necessary blade tension, insert the blade into the top

FIG. 2–5   Disc cutter. *Courtesy of Allcraft.*

clamp and tighten the clamp. Then adjust the height of the saw frame so that the free end of the blade rests about one-half of the way down on the bottom clamp. Slip the blade through the drilled hole and rest the metal at the top of the saw blade. Using one hand to guide the blade into the bottom clamp and your chest and other hand to apply pressure, press the top end of the saw frame against the workbench (figure 2–6). When there is sufficient pressure to make the blade reach the bottom of the clamp, tighten the clamp with the blade in place inside the bottom clamp. At this point the blade should be taut enough to ring with a high pitch when plucked.

The best position for sawing is at chest level. Avoid back and neck strain by finding a stool and workbench of a comfortable height. Good lighting will prevent eyestrain.

Before you begin sawing, you may want to lubricate the saw blade with beeswax or soap, being careful not to clog the teeth. Then hold the metal firmly on the V-board with one hand, and with the other hand draw the saw up and down at right angles to the metal (figure 2–7). To saw a curved line, gradually turn metal or saw. Breakage may occur if the angle of the blade is changed, if the metal is not braced firmly against the V-board, or if too much pressure is exerted on the blade. Beginners will break many blades before sawing becomes second nature. Broken blades that are long enough to permit sawing may be used again by adjusting the frame to accommodate the smaller size.

Filing

When the sawing is completed, you are ready to file your work in order to refine the shape and texture of the edges and surfaces. Files come in many shapes, cuts, and sizes (figure 2–8). The

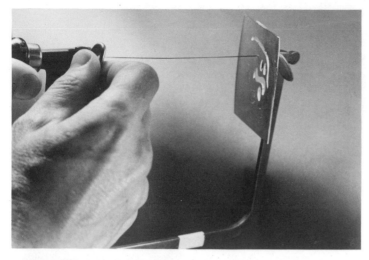

FIG. 2–6   Thread the metal on the saw blade and tighten the blade, under tension, in the lower clamp.

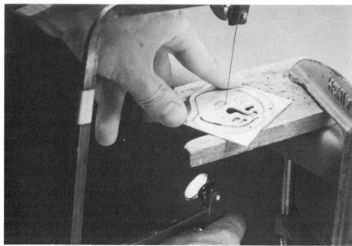

FIG. 2–7   Saw out the metal forms, holding the blade perpendicular to the metal. Brace the work on a V-board.

smallest files, called needle files, are helpful in getting to small areas (figure 2–9). Round and half-round files will smooth concave forms, whereas flat files are used for convex and flat forms. Other shapes are available for specific needs. (See the table of *Dixon Grobet Swiss Precision Files* on p. 207.)

Use progressively finer files to reduce gradually the size of file marks and scratches. Begin with a coarse or medium-cut file and work down to a fine file. Keep your file clean with a wire brush.

Hold the file with your forefinger stretched out on top of the file and the rest of your hand around the base. Support the metal on a bench pin, and file flat across the top of the piece to remove any deep scratches (figure 2–10). To preserve the file and use the least amount of effort, always apply pressure on the forward stroke, in the direction away from the file handle and away from your body.

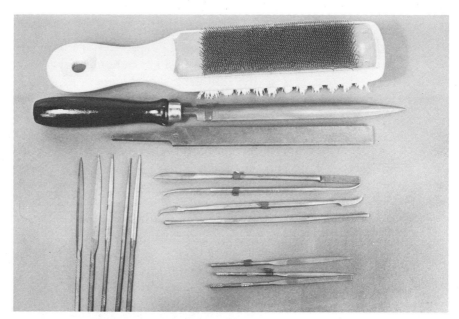

FIG. 2–8   Files. From top: File cleaner, hand files, riffle files, small needle files. Lower left: Needle files.

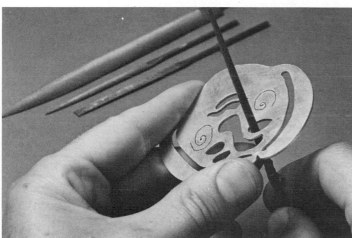

FIG. 2–9   File small areas with needle files of the appropriate shapes.

FIG. 2–10   Supporting the metal on a bench pin, file to remove any deep scratches.

Sanding and Hand Polishing

Like filing, sanding is accomplished with progressively finer grit emery papers (figure 2–11). Sanding removes all traces of file marks. Use the following emery papers in succession to refine the metal surface: 240, 320, 400, and 600 grits, and finally crocus cloth. To use the emery paper, wrap it around a sanding stick made from a 1″ × 10″ (2.5 × 25 cm) piece of wood or a plastic sanding stick purchased from a jewelry supply house (figure 2–12).

Polishing compounds may be used to achieve a highly polished finish. The first polishing compound to use is tripoli. For an even higher polish, use rouge after the tripoli. To apply the compound, rub it onto a stick buff, either purchased or constructed from a 1″ × 10″ (2.5 × 25 cm) stick to which a strip of felt has been glued (figure 2–13). Use a separate stick buff for each compound. In addition, when switching polishing compounds, clean the metal beforehand in warm water to which a dash of detergent and ammonia has been added.

Other polishing techniques you may wish to consider include Scotch stoning and burnishing. Scotch stone may be purchased in a thin stick form and is an excellent abrasive for hard-to-reach areas. The stone may be sanded to a point or other shape to fit a specific spot. The resulting matt finish may be left as the final surface, or the surface may be polished as explained above.

A highly polished steel burnishing tool may also be rubbed over the metal surface to achieve a high polish. This tool is especially useful in polishing small areas. (A burnisher is shown in figure 3–8).

Attaching the Pendant to the Chain

A simple way to attach the pendant to the neck chain is with jump rings, as shown in figure 2–1. Jump rings and chains may be purchased at a jewelry supply store or they may be handcrafted, as described in Chapter 7. Select a size appropriate to your piece. Depending on size, balance, and style, one or more jump rings are required.

Using a drill, pierce holes in the pendant to accomodate the jump rings. To open a ring, use two pliers to twist the ends in opposite directions (figure 2–14). Do not attempt to open the rings by spreading the ends apart. Insert the open ring(s) in the pierced hole(s). Then close the rings with pliers, twisting the metal back to its original shape.

FIG. 2–11   Materials for hand polishing. From left: plastic polishing stick, emery papers, crocus cloth, and polishing compounds (tripoli and rouge).

FIG. 2–12   Sand the surface of the metal with progressively finer grit emery papers attached to the sanding stick.

FIG. 2–13   Polish with a polishing stick.

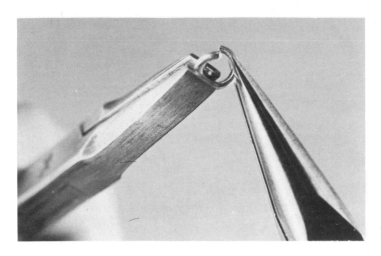

FIG. 2–14 To open and close jump rings, twist rather than spreading the ends apart.

Soldering Tools

Soldering is one of several methods of joining metals. In soldering, two pieces of metal are heated with a torch and joined by a metal alloy that melts at a lower temperature than the metals being joined.

Solders

The most commonly used solders for jewelry work are silver and gold. Silver solder is used for silver, brass, bronze, copper, nickel silver, gold, and almost any metal that has a melting point above that of the solder. Aluminum, however, cannot be soldered with silver solder. Silver solder, an alloy of silver (anywhere from 15 to 80 percent), copper, and zinc, is available in different grades (melting points) to facilitate successive soldering operations on a single piece. Solders vary according to the temperature at which they flow: from easy-flo (1145°F, 618°C) through easy (1325°F, 718°C), medium (1390°F, 754°C), and hard (1425°F, 774°C), to IT solder (1460°F, 793°C). (These temperatures vary slightly depending on the manufacturer.) IT solder is used primarily in enameling to prevent soldered joints from flowing at enameling kiln temperatures. Easy-flo solder, with its low melting point, is used mainly for repair work. Most silver soldering is done with easy-, medium-, and hard-grade solders. In a multiple soldering operation, the harder solder is used first because it will not reflow when the next soldering is done with a lower grade solder. On a piece that is soldered three times, for example, you would use hard, then medium, and then easy solder. (For precautions when soldering, see Chapter 11.)

Gold solder is available in a variety of grades and colors made to match the gold in the piece to be soldered.

All grades of solder should be carefully labeled and kept separate from one another to ensure availability of the correct solder for a specific purpose.

Forms of Solder

Solder comes in wire, sheet, rod, paste, and powder form. Wire and sheet solder are the most common forms used in jewelry making, and they are the only forms called for in this book. Wire may be cut into $\frac{1}{16}''$ (2 mm) pieces or used directly from the coil (stick soldering). Better placement and control of uncut wire may be achieved by threading the end of the coil through a section of close-fitting tubing. This tube acts as a soldering pen through which the solder is fed as it is used. (Such an arrangement is shown in use in figure 2–35.)

Sheet solder must be cut into tiny pieces, approximately $\frac{1}{32}''$ (1 mm) square. This is best accomplished by making close parallel cuts with bezel shears. Then, as solder is needed, make cross cuts (figure 2–15). These chips of solder are called *paillons*. Powdered solder is made from solder filings and is used most commonly in filigree work. Paste solder contains flux.

Fluxing

The area of metal to be soldered must remain free of dirt and oxides, or else the soldering will not be successful. Cleaning and protecting the metal is accomplished by fluxing. An entire piece may be coated with flux to help prevent firescale, a black oxide that occurs upon heating any metal that contains copper (such as sterling silver). Solder, too, should be fluxed before use.

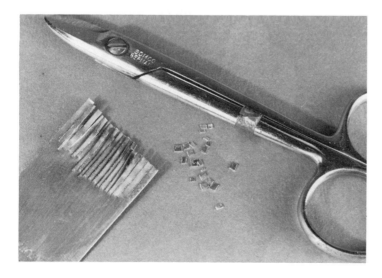

FIG. 2–15 Cut paillons of solder with bezel shears.

Hard-solder flux, which is used in jewelry making operations, comes in paste and liquid forms. It is applied either with a small brush or sprayed on. Handy Flux is one commercially prepared flux that is used by many jewelers. Borax is often used as a flux in casting.

For precautions when using flux, see page 204.

Soldering Torches

The heat used in soldering is supplied by a torch. Torches vary according to the size of the flame, the type of gas, and the temperature produced. Portability may also be a factor to consider when choosing a torch.

A small propane torch with a disposable tank is inexpensive and portable, and it may be used for soldering operations where intense heat is not required (figure 2–16). Most operations described in this book can be accomplished using the propane torch. Large projects and some special techniques require a hotter flame. The propane torch may be fitted with a rubber hose for convenient handling. Always hold the torch in the weaker hand so that your stronger hand will be available for precision work.

A more versatile torch is the acetylene gas torch (figure 2–17). Air is drawn through the handpiece and combines with the gas from the tank. These refillable tanks are larger than those used in the propane torch and in the long run are more economical for the jeweler who intends to use larger quantities of gas. A number of different size tips are available that allow variations in the size of the flame. The Prest-O-Lite B tank (40 cu. ft. capacity, or 1,360 liters) is a good size for most jewelry shops.

Two other types of torch used by jewelers are gas-air and oxygen-gas torches. Each torch has two valves to adjust the amount of gas and oxygen or air (figure 2–18). The natural gas-air torch gives a highly controllable and versatile flame and is an excellent all-purpose torch. Its major limitation is that it can be used only where natural gas is available. Compressed air is used with this torch.

An intensely hot flame may be gotten from the oxygen-acetylene torch, used mainly where intense heat is called for. The oxygen makes the flame hotter. Other gases, such as natural and propane, may also be used in conjunction with oxygen in order to increase their temperatures.

The following precautions should be taken when using a torch:
• Before using your tank, check for leaks at all joints by applying soapy water and watching for bubbles. Store a leaky tank outdoors until it can be returned to the manufacturer for repair.
• Never store a gas tank in a confined space.

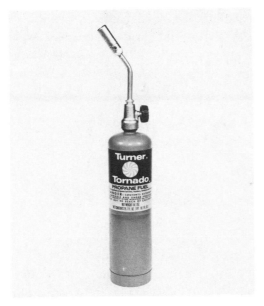

FIG. 2–16   Propane torch with
a disposable tank. *Courtesy of
Allcraft.*

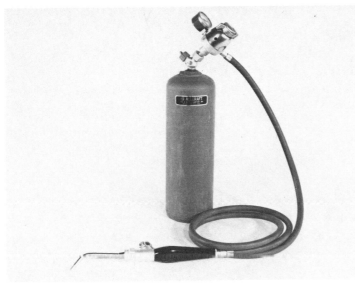

FIG. 2–17   Prest-O-Lite torch
(acetylene gas). *Courtesy of
Allcraft.*

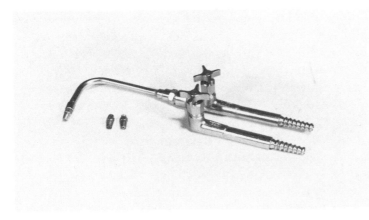

FIG. 2–18   Oxygen-gas torch,
which hooks up via hoses to
tanks of oxygen and gas.
Courtesy of Allcraft.

- Keep tanks away from heat and fire.
- Handle with care. Do not drop the tank.
- Keep the tank upright and held in a stand or chained to a stable object.
- Close the cylinder valves and empty gas from the hose after working.
- Work in a well-ventilated area.

Soldering Surfaces

The best surfaces on which to solder do not conduct heat but rather help to concentrate it around the piece. One such surface is a charcoal block. Another is an annealing pan filled with pumice lumps. The lumps may be used to prop an oddly shaped piece while soldering, and they allow the heat to flow under the metal. An annealing pan may be purchased from a jewelry supply store or made from a hubcap or wok. A tripod with a wire mesh top is excellent for holding a piece high enough to allow the heat to be directed from below.

Firebrick may be used to cover a tabletop or soldering area. Soft asbestos is a health hazard and should *never* be used; hard asbestos (transite) can be used because it is less likely to flake. (For further discussion of asbestos and its substitutes, see page 202.)

Pickling

In order for soldering and other processes to be effective, it is essential that the metals involved be thoroughly clean. Metal is cleaned by pickling. Pickle is an acid solution that removes oxides, flux, grease, and dirt from the metal. One pickling solution, Sparex, is used by many jewelers and is safer than using sulfuric or nitric acid. (For precautions when using acids, see page 203.)

Heating the pickle solution will hasten the cleaning process. An electric, ceramic-lined slow cooker is an excellent container in which to keep the pickle warm, and it is less expensive than the electric pickling pot sold specifically for this purpose. Pickle may also be heated in a covered Pyrex container over a hot plate. Care should be taken not to boil the pickle, however.

Soak the metal in the pickle until it is clean. Use only copper, stainless steel or brass tongs to remove metal from the solution. Never introduce iron or steel into this solution; these metals will cause metal surfaces to become copper coated. Avoid fumes and skin contact by allowing hot metal to air cool until the redness disappears before immersing it into the pickling solution. Close the lid immediately after use. To neutralize pickle trapped within hollow forms such as beads, boil in a solution of baking soda and water.

Butt Soldering: Making a Bangle Bracelet

Butt soldering is a technique used to join two pieces of wire or sheet metal that meet end to end without overlapping.

Materials. Triangular wire $^3/_{16}''$ (5 mm) base $\times$ 8″ (20.3 cm) long, jeweler's saw, file, needle files, bracelet mandrel, mallet, soldering and polishing materials, liver of sulfur (potassium sulfide), Q-tip.

Soldering Materials. Torch; striker; soldering surfaces (transite, charcoal block, annealing pan, and tripod with wire mesh); soldering pick; easy, medium, and hard solder; flux and a small brush; pickle and copper or stainless steel tongs; water in a flat pan; tweezers. See figure 2–19.

Cutting and Cleaning the Wire

Begin to make the bangle bracelet by cutting an 8″ (20.5 cm) length of $^3/_{16}''$ (5 mm) base triangular wire with a jeweler's saw. File the ends of the wire flat until they meet squarely when the wire has

FIG. 2–19   Materials for soldering.

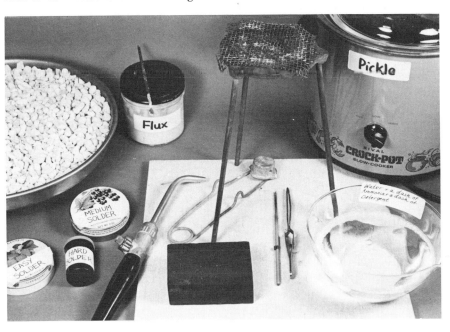

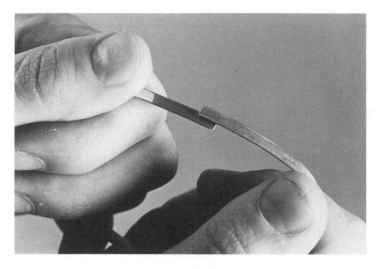

FIG. 2–20 Spring the wire so that the ends will meet squarely by pushing them past each other.

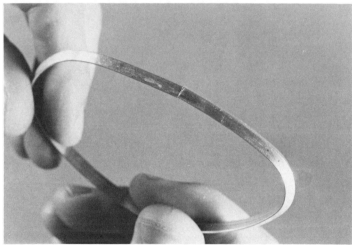

FIG. 2–21 The tension on the wire allows the ends to spring together and hold for soldering.

been bent into a circle. A crooked joint will make soldering difficult and may result in a weak connection.

In order to solder effectively, it is essential that the metal surfaces be thoroughly clean. Clean the wire either by immersing it in pickle and rinsing in water, or by washing it in soap and warm water, or by rubbing it clean with fine steel wool or emery paper.

Springing the Wire

When the metal is clean and the ends of the wire meet in a perfect joint, they are sprung together in order to create tension on the joint. This is done by pushing the ends of the wire past one another and snapping them back together (figure 2–20). The tension thus created will keep the ends from spreading apart while soldering (figure 2–21).

Soldering

Since only one soldering operation will be necessary, easy solder will be used. First brush flux over the wire bracelet and the solder and place the bracelet on the soldering surface. Hold the wire in position with tweezers. Apply paillons of solder or cut wire across the inner surface of the joint with a small brush. For this small joint, very little solder is needed. Beginners often use too much solder and then have to spend a great deal of time filing the piece.

For the solder to flow and adhere, the metal must reach the flow temperature of the solder. Use your torch to heat the metal rather than the solder, since the thin solder will reach the proper temperature quicker than the metal. Keep the flame at a distance from the metal so that the inner cone of the flame is near but not touching it (figure 2–22).

If the solder is not jumping (filling) a seam, but rather is running up one side only, coax it along with a soldering pick, as shown in figure 2–22. This pick may be purchased or made from a length of coat-hanger wire that has been filed to a point at one end. The pick is used to give the solder a push in the right direction and to break the surface tension, allowing it to flow more easily.

Remember that solder will flow toward the hottest point, so heat the side of the seam to which you want the solder to flow. Determining the exact placement of the flame and the amount of heat needed takes experience. After the solder has flowed, remove the torch immediately to prevent the metal from overheating and melting.

Pickling and Filing

After the soldered bracelet has cooled for a few seconds, immerse it in the warm pickle (figure 2–23). Pickling when the metal is too hot

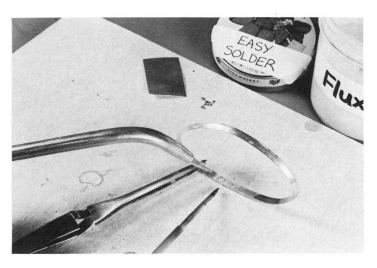

FIG. 2–22 Butt solder the joint, using a soldering pick to help direct the solder.

may place undue stress on the metal and may also produce noxious fumes. After the bracelet is clean, rinse it in water.

Now file off any excess solder (figure 2–24). Little filing is necessary if you have soldered correctly. File marks are removed with emery paper (240, 320, 400, and 600 grits). After filing, there should be no sign of the soldered joint.

Shaping and Decorative Finishing

After you have butt soldered, filed, and emeried the bracelet, round it on a bracelet mandrel. A tapered steel bracelet mandrel may be purchased or one may be improvised from a rolling pin or a baseball bat.

Slip the bracelet over the mandrel and push it down the taper until it forms a perfect circle. Use a mallet to shape the bracelet

FIG. 2–23   Pickle the metal.

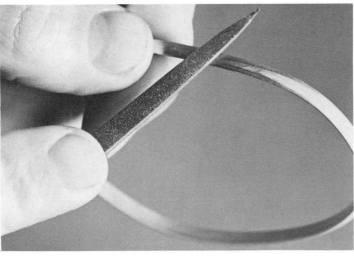

FIG. 2–24   File off excess solder until there is no evidence of a soldered joint.

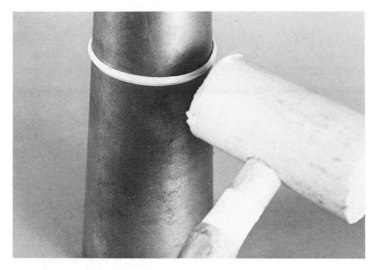

FIG. 2–25   Place the bracelet on a bracelet mandrel and use a mallet to round it.

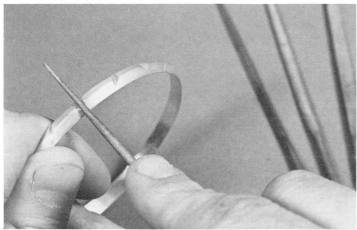

FIG. 2–26   Use various needle files to create decorative grooves in the triangular wire.

because the soft wood or rawhide will not stretch or dent the metal, as would a hammer (figure 2–25). Next, remove the bracelet from the mandrel, lay it on a flat metal or wood surface, and hit it flat on both sides with the mallet. Return the bracelet to the mandrel and repeat the process until the bracelet is flat and round.

To add decoration, use assorted needle files to shape grooves into the triangular wire (figure 2–26). Do not file deeply or you may weaken the bracelet. Emery and polish by hand or by machine. (Instructions for machine polishing follow.)

Coloring with Liver of Sulfur

Liver of sulfur (potassium sulfide) is an excellent coloring agent for silver and can produce surface colors ranging through the entire spectrum. However, the chemical is highly toxic, so always wear a respirator and have good ventilation whenever using it.

If you have made your bracelet of silver, after you have emeried and polished it, you may wish to emphasize your filed design by darkening the metal with liver of sulfur. Allowing the oxide to remain within the grooves while polishing off any surface oxide will highlight your design and create contrast. A black surface may be obtained be keeping the metal in the solution for a longer period of time. Heating the liver of sulfur will hasten the darkening process.

Make a solution by dissolving a small lump of liver of sulfur in a cup of hot water. It is best always to use a fresh solution, for it deteriorates quickly when exposed to air. To achieve the desired color, dip the piece into the solution, quickly remove it, and rinse it in running water. Continue doing this until the metal reaches the desired color. Fix the final color by rinsing the piece in water to which a dash of detergent and ammonia has been added.

Selected areas may be colored by applying the liver of sulfur with a Q-tip (figure 2–27). Remove the sulfide where not desired by rubbing the area with powdered pumice or polish the area by hand or machine. A lovely finish may be achieved by rubbing the colored metal with a brass brush dipped in water containing detergent and ammonia.

Polishing by Machine

A polishing machine consists of a small one-half or one-third horsepower motor with one or two tapered spindles to which buffs, wheels, and brushes may be attached (figure 2–28). A hood fitted with a light will trap dust around the machine. In addition, an electrically operated dust-collecting system is advisable to reduce

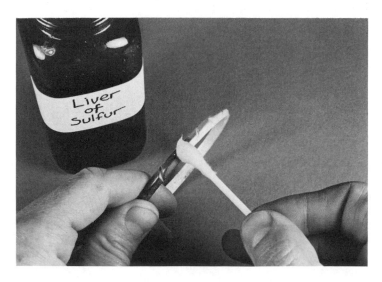

FIG. 2–27   Darken the grooves for contrast with liver of sulfur.

FIG. 2–28 Polishing machine. *Courtesy of Allcraft.*

the amount of dust in the air. Used motors are readily available and can be purchased at flea markets, garage sales, and junk stores.

For buffing and polishing, a speed of around 3,500 rpm is desirable. The larger the polishing buff, the more buffing a piece will receive at any particular speed. Thus the "speed" of a slow machine may be increased by using large buffs.

There are almost as many methods of polishing as there are jewelers. The speed, type of compounds used, and type of buffs are all variable. Individual preference is arrived at through experimentation. One jeweler's method is presented here.

Goggles and a respirator with a dust filter should be worn at all times when buffing and polishing.

Materials.   Emery paper (240, 320, 400, and 600 grits), polishing machine with hood, 2 muslin buffs, felt ring buff, goggles, respirator with dust filter, tripoli, rouge, bowl with water and a dash of detergent and ammonia. See figure 2–29.

Buffing

The metal is ready to be buffed after it has been emeried with 240, 320, 400, and 600 grit emery paper. Buffing removes the scratches left by the emery.

To buff, use tripoli on a muslin buff. Bobbing, a rather rough polishing compound, is sometimes applied with a bristle brush prior to tripoli for quick cutting, but care must be taken not to remove so much metal that you distort the surface. Apply the tripoli by holding it against the moving buff, and recharge the buff when necessary. Do not overcharge the buff or it will clog and become ineffective. If this should occur, the buff may be raked. A rake may be con-

FIG. 2–29   Materials for polishing by machine.

structed from a board through which nails have been driven until they protrude. A knife may also be used for this purpose. The rake is held against the buff until it rakes out the dirt.

Hold the work in both hands at the bottom of the buff. The buff should spin downward and toward you (figure 2–30), so any work that is dropped will be flung into the hood. A leather glove or fingers may be worn to protect the hands from heat created by friction.

Use a separate buff for each compound, and label buffs in order to prevent mixing of compounds. Between compounds, wash your

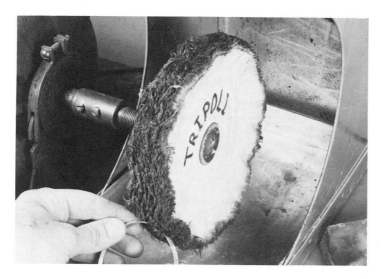

FIG. 2–30   Hold the metal in both hands at the bottom front of the buff, with the buff spinning downward and toward you.

work in water to which a dash of detergent and ammonia has been added.

Buffing removes all scratches from the surface, and polishing is necessary only if a high shine is desired. Many jewelers prefer the slightly muted finish that tripoli leaves. Figure 2–31 shows the finished bracelet, which has been buffed and polished.

Polishing

For a high polish, rouge is used on a muslin buff. The rouge will subtly affect the color of the metal. Red rouge is often used on warm-colored metals, including silver. Black, white, yellow, and green rouge are also available. Polishing is done the same way as buffing. Wash the piece again after polishing.

The Flexible Shaft

The flexible shaft (figure 2–32) is useful for holding a variety of miniature accessories used in texturing, grinding, drilling, buffing, and polishing. These accessories are available in many shapes and are excellent for working on small and hard-to-reach areas.

Sweat Soldering: Making a Belt Buckle

Sweat soldering is a technique used to solder one sheet of metal on top of another. The solder is placed between the two sheets and heat is applied mainly from beneath the work. Wire mesh on a tripod is used to support the work while soldering.

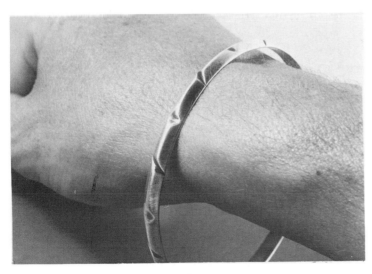

FIG. 2–31   Completed bangle bracelet.

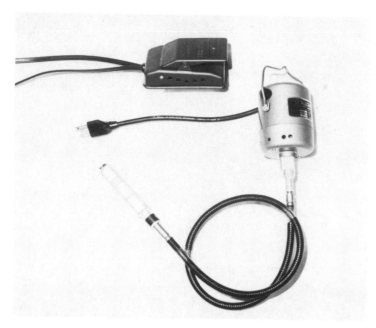

FIG. 2–32   The flexible shaft.
Courtesy of Allcraft.

Materials.   Two sheets of 18-gauge metal of the same or contrasting colors, 10-gauge round wire, rawhide or wooden mallet, jeweler's saw, needle files, file, steel surface plate, metal shears, soldering materials, round-nose pliers, and polishing materials.

The Buckle

The belt buckle in figure 2–33 is made from two layers of metal. The top layer is pierced and the bottom layer is left solid. The layers will be soldered together to produce a single piece of metal.

After piercing, both sheets are flattened with a wooden or rawhide mallet, working against a flat, hard surface, such as a steel surface plate (figure 2–34). When the sheets are flat and fit together without gaps, pickle and flux the entire piece.

Soldering the Layers

Working on wire mesh mounted on a tripod, apply wire solder from the coil or sheet solder paillons to the bottom surface of the pierced sheet (figure 2–35). Heat the metal until the solder melts. If you are using uncut wire solder straight from the coil, apply a test piece first. When this melts, add solder. Use a soldering pick to spread the solder over the entire surface. Do not use more solder than is necessary to cover the sheets with a thin layer of melted solder.

FIG. 2–33　Pierced top, bottom plate, and findings are soldered together to make the belt buckle.

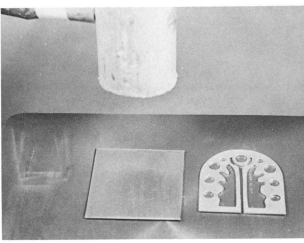

FIG. 2–34　Use a mallet to flatten the metal sheets against a surface plate.

FIG. 2–35　Apply the solder to cover the back of the pierced sheet.

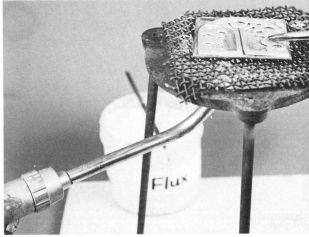

FIG. 2–36　Solder the solder-covered pierced sheet to the base by applying heat mainly from below.

When the solder is melted and spread, allow the piece to cool sufficiently for the solder to freeze. Position the upper, pierced sheet onto the base sheet. Using a torch, heat the piece from below, watching the edges for the solder to flow (Figure 2–36). If gaps are visible, solder may be added to the edges of the base where it meets the top piece. When the solder flows, push the upper, pierced sheet down in contact with the base with a soldering pick or tweezers.

Remove the heat source and let the solder freeze and the piece cool for a few seconds before immersing it in the pickle. Rinse in

FIG. 2–37 Cutting tools. From top: Wire cutters, bezel shears, plate shears, aviation snips.

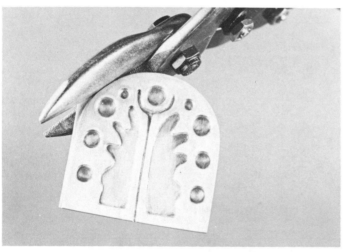

FIG. 2–38 Cut excess metal with shears.

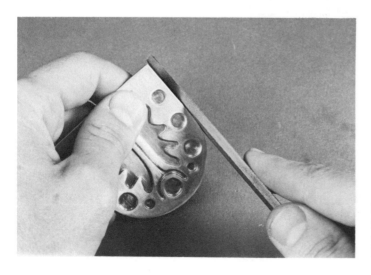

FIG. 2–39 File the edges so that the top and bottom pieces fit perfectly together and appear to be a single piece.

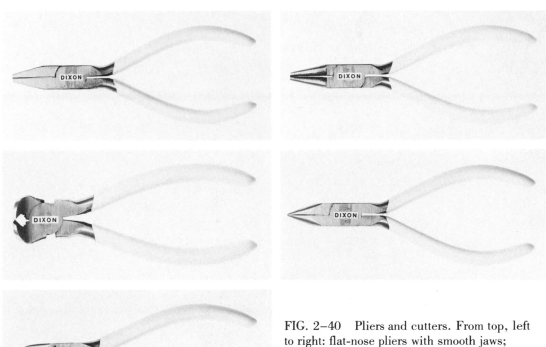

FIG. 2–40 Pliers and cutters. From top, left to right: flat-nose pliers with smooth jaws; round-nose pliers with smooth, tapered jaws; end nippers with close-cutting jaws; chain-nose pliers with smooth, tapered jaws; side cutter with pointed tips. *Courtesy of William Dixon Company.*

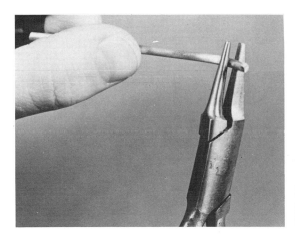

FIG. 2–41 Bend the wire with pliers to make the findings for the belt buckle.

water. Now you are ready to cut excess metal with shears (figure 2–37) and file any rough edges to create the appearance of a single thickness of metal (figures 2–38 and 2–39). Removing any excess solder from the edges of the pierced holes can be a problem. Scotch stone filed to a point or riffle files can help. It is best simply not to use too much solder in the first place.

FIG. 2–42 Melt the solder onto the ends of the findings to prepare them for soldering to the back of the buckle.

FIG. 2–43 Solder the findings to the back of the buckle.

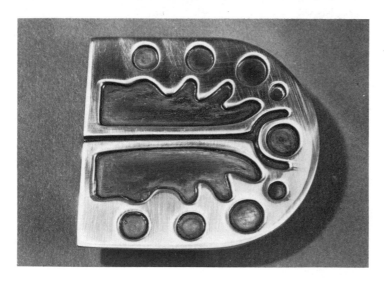

FIG. 2–44 Completed belt buckle.

Shaping the Buckle Findings

The findings for this belt buckle (the hook and the strap holder) are made with two pieces of 10-gauge round wire. The strap holder is measured to the width of the buckle, plus approximately ½″ (1.3 cm) for the thickness of the belt and filing. The smaller piece, used as a hook to insert into the belt hole, should measure approximately ⅝″ (1.5 cm). Cut the wire with a shears or saw.

To make the findings, begin by bending the longer piece of wire in a shallow U to fit the buckle, as shown in (figure 2–41). Forming or round-nose pliers are used to bend the wire (figure 2–40). The hook is made by bending the small piece of wire into an L shape (figure 2–33) and filing it to a dull point at one end. Next, file the three remaining ends of the two pieces of wire flat so that they lie flush with the buckle. Pickle and flux all pieces to prepare for soldering.

Soldering and Finishing

Using tweezers to hold each wire, place a generous amount of solder next to and touching the three ends of the wires (figure 2–42). As you heat the wire, the solder will flow towards and adhere to the wire.

When solder has been applied to the wires, heat the buckle until it reaches soldering temperature. Handy Flux may be used as a temperature indicator. At soldering temperature, the flux will turn clear. Another method used to indicate temperature is to place a small chip of solder on the metal and watch for it to flow. (Solder will melt but not flow until the metal is hot enough.) Because of the difference in size between the wire findings and the sheet metal that forms the main section of the piece, a great deal more heat will be needed to bring the sheet metal up to soldering temperature. So direct the flame primarily to the buckle.

When soldering the findings onto the base, remember that solder will flow to the hottest area. Therefore, in order to make the solder flow from the wires down to the buckle, the flame should be directed onto the buckle and away from the wires. When the strap holder is soldered in place, solder the hook facing inward toward the strap holder (figure 2–43).

Next, file, emery, and polish the buckle. A belt may be stitched, riveted, or macramed onto the buckle. The finished buckle is shown in figure 2–44.

Dimension: Forging and Relief

3

This chapter explores several techniques for creating depth and dimension in wire and sheet metal. These techniques include forging, dapping, die forming, repoussé, and chasing. Before any of these techniques can be applied, though, the metal must be annealed in order to make it softer and easier to work.

Annealing

When working on nonferrous metals (those that do not contain iron), the internal structure of the metal changes as the metal is hammered, filed, bent, rolled, or otherwise worked. This is known as *work-hardening*, and when it occurs, the metal gradually becomes more springy and brittle. At times this spring and hardness is desirable. However, too much stress can cause the metal to crack, requiring a difficult and time-consuming repair job. In order to prevent undue stress, the metal must be annealed whenever it has been worked to a point of brittleness and no longer responds easily to working. This can happen many times.

To anneal, the metal is heated with a torch to a temperature at which its internal structure is "relaxed." This makes the metal soft and workable again. The time it takes to anneal is only a matter of minutes. Overheating beyond the annealing temperature must be avoided.

Metals change colors when heated, so color is a good indicator for determining temperature. Annealing temperature for yellow, red, and green gold and sterling silver occurs at dull red; brass is heated to light red; and copper, bronze, NuGold, and white gold are heated to cherry red.

When annealing thin wire, wind it in a coil to prevent melting and uneven annealing. It is easy to melt sections of uncoiled wire. With sheet metal play the flame over the whole surface to heat evenly. Always heat in an annealing pan or other heat-proof surface.

After heating, most metals are quenched in water or in a pickle solution. Allow sterling silver, brass, and white gold to cool until the redness disappears before putting them into the pickle or water. Red gold should be quenched immediately. There are, however, many different theories about quenching and its effect on metals. Each jeweler should experiment and discover her or his personal preference.

DESIGNING YOUR WORK: LINE IN SPACE

We see the lines of a tree branch against the sky, vines spiraling upward, telephone wires crisscrossed, scribbling and writing, roads on a map. We respond to line traveling through space and time as to a dance or melody. A line has energy and direction. Like a path in the woods, it takes the eye on a journey along its length. A slowly curving line is calmer than a sharp, angular line. A line can be nervous, bold, or tentative. Thus our visual references may influence us when we design a forged piece of jewelry.

Forging: Making a Fibula

Forging is a technique used to form metal and create variation in thickness by hammering the metal against an anvil or a flat or curved steel surface. Forging hammers come in a variety of shapes and sizes for particular jobs. The pressure of the hammer thins the metal at the point of impact and pushes the metal outward, stretching and spreading it. Because forging involves much stress, it is important to anneal the metal frequently to prevent it from becoming work-hardened.

Materials. 10-gauge (or thicker) square wire, 3 ½" (9 cm) or longer; surface plate; mallet; cross-peen and planishing hammers; wet and dry emery papers (240, 320, 400, and 600 grits); assorted needle files; half-round medium-cut file; pliers; burnishers; annealing equipment.

When you begin to forge wire, experiment first. Working with a piece of square 8- or 10-gauge wire and hammering against a steel surface plate, try forging the wire to different thicknesses. Hold the hammer at different angles in relation to the metal to see how to make a smooth or textured surface. Work with cross-peen and planishing hammers and observe how the metal moves. See what happens when you forge the wire too thin and when overlapping

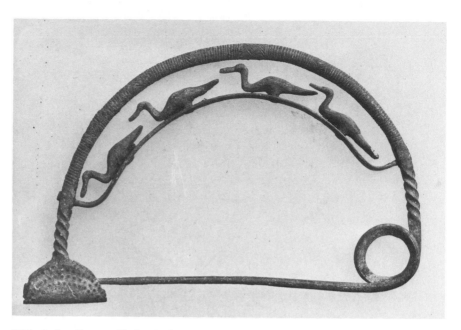

FIG. 3–1 Bronze fibula. Italic. C. 1350–1050 B. C. The Metropolitan Museum of Art, Fletcher Fund, 1926.

wires are forged. Try making gentle, tight, angular, or flowing curves.

Shaping the Pin

The fibula is an ancient form of jewelry that resembles an ornamental safety pin. An antique fibula is shown in figure 3–1. The finished fibula described in this project is shown in figure 3–9.

Most wire is annealed before it is sold. However, it is always best to anneal it again before you begin forging (figure 3–2). Start by thinning and lengthening the section of wire that will become the pin stem. This will be approximately 1½" (3.8 cm) if you are using 10-gauge wire. This will allow enough wire for a loop, which will act as a spring for the pin stem. Note that as the wire is thinned, its length increases (figure 3–3). Thick wire must be thinned a great deal at the pin stem, and it will consequently greatly increase in length.

To forge the pin stem, use a cross-peen hammer (see figure 3–4), working against a smooth steel surface plate. The hammer, when held perpendicular to the wire, will move the wire in a direction along its length (figure 3–5). Any dents in the surface plate or hammer will be transferred to the metal, so be certain that you work against a smooth area unless texture is desired.

Forge the pin stem by tapering the square wire along the 1½"

FIG. 3–2 Anneal and pickle the metal before you begin to forge.

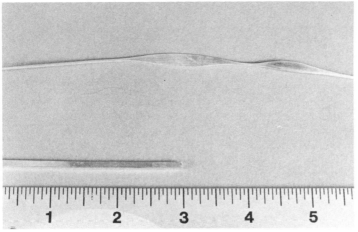

FIG. 3–3 A 3″ length (7.6 cm) of 10-gauge square wire is forged to 6″ (15.2 cm).

(3.8 cm) length. Turn the wire over on the opposite side and repeat. Next, hammer the remaining two sides in succession, keeping the wire square and the edges straight. If necessary, the edges may be straightened by gentle hammering. When the edges begin to mushroom out and the metal becomes resistant to hammering, it is time to anneal.

As you proceed, the wire may begin to curve. To prevent it from curving to one side, hold the hammer straight. If the hammer is held at an angle, one side of the wire will be hit harder than the other and will cause the wire to bend away from the side with the greater stretch. If this occurs, hammer the opposite side of the wire with greater force until the wire straightens. It takes practice to be able to keep the wire straight and free of hammer dents.

A mallet may also be used to flatten a gentle curve in the wire. It can be made from rawhide, rubber, plastic, or wood and because each is softer than the metal, it will not spread or dent the metal as would a hammer.

Next, thin and taper approximately ½″ (1.3 cm) of the opposite end of the wire in the same manner. This will later be filed round and bent to make the hook.

To spread the wire flat in areas to make up the design on the pin face, use a planishing hammer (see figures 3–4 and 3–6). The slightly convex head of the planishing hammer will spread the metal in all directions, widening and lengthening it at the same time.

Be careful not to hammer the metal too thin or it may eventually break. Forging overlapping wires may also weaken the piece, since the wires, at the point of intersection, will cut into each other and become thin.

FIG. 3–4   Hammers. From top, left to right: forming, ball-peen, rivet, chasing, cross-peen, planishing.

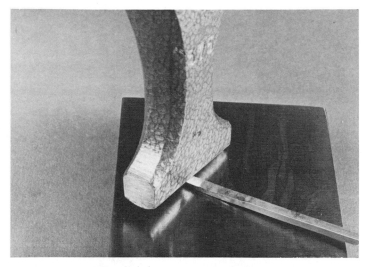

FIG. 3–5   Use a cross-peen hammer to stretch the metal along its length.

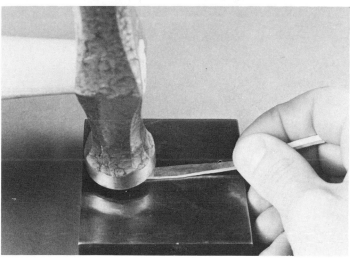

FIG. 3–6   Use a planishing hammer to spread the metal in all directions.

Refining the Form.

When you have finished forging, file the wire to refine the form of your line. File the pin stem round and to a fine point and test it in a piece of fabric. It should enter easily and should not leave a large hole. Use course files at the start and progress to finer files until the metal is ready to be emeried and burnished.

Bending the Wire

Anneal the wire to make it flexible for bending. Then bend it into the desired shape by using forming or round-nose pliers for curved bends and flat-nose pliers for angular bends (figure 3–7). One set of pliers may be used in conjunction with another or with your free

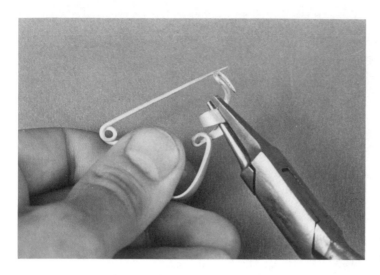

FIG. 3–7   Bend the formed wire with a pliers. Note the pin stem, hook, and spring.

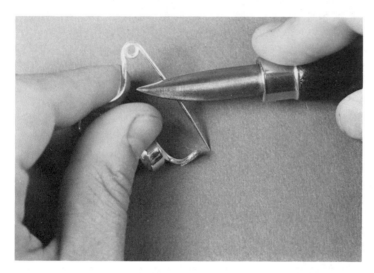

FIG. 3–8   Rub the metal surface with a burnisher.

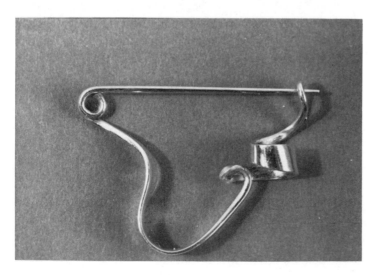

FIG. 3–9   Completed forged fibula.

hand. To avoid plier dents in the metal, do not grip the pliers too tightly. Wherever possible, bend simple curves with your hands. When bending the wire, twist it around into a loop just before the stem. This will create the necessary tension and spring for the pin. At the opposite end of the pin, bend a hook out of the wire to lock the pin stem in place.

Finishing

Finish the surface by using progressively finer emery paper (240 to 600 grits) and then a burnisher. The highly polished burnisher will leave a shine on the surface when it is rubbed over the metal (figure 3–8).

Forged Wire Variations

Two wires can be made from one by sawing a wire down the middle. A figure can be made by splitting a wire at both ends, the split ends becoming the arms and legs. In the piece shown in figure 3–10, a pearl head was added by gluing the pearl, drilled with a single hole in one end, onto the tapered end of a wire soldered to the torso. Epoxy glue was used to attach the pearl to the wire.

A simple choker can be made from round wire that is forged with a planishing hammer (figure 3–11). If a rolling mill is available (see figure 5–10), try tapering and thinning the wire, using the mill rather than the hammer.

DESIGNING YOUR WORK: DIMENSION IN RELIEF

Relief is a type of sculpture in which the forms project above or below a plane. Whereas sculpture-in-the-round can be viewed from all angles, relief sculpture is primarily viewed from the front. The methods in this chapter describe relief techniques that can be applied to jewelry making.

Light plays an important role in relief sculpture. As the angle at which light hits the raised and lowered surfaces changes, the shadows change in value and size. Jewelry is a unique form of sculpture because it is displayed on a person and is often in motion. The illusion of greater or lesser depth within the relief constantly changes.

Some of the most successful relief sculptures display many levels within a single work. Working from the surface plane, you can project in either direction to create great dimensional variety within a small space.

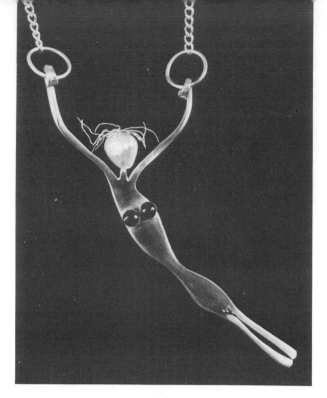

FIG. 3–10 Pendant made from square wire that was split with a jeweler's saw and forged.

FIG. 3–11 Choker made from round wire that was forged over a textured surface using a planishing hammer.

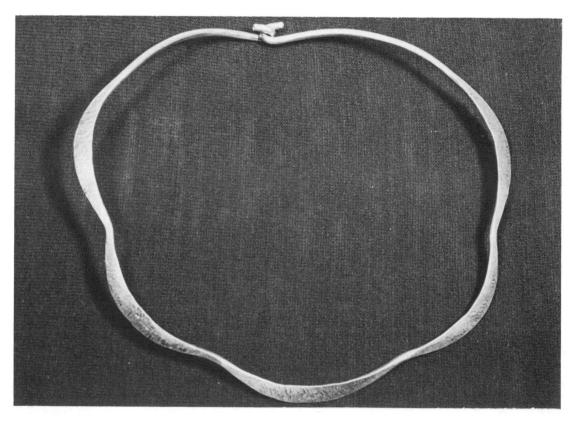

Dapping: The Dome as a Decorative Element

One method of creating dimension in jewelry is by using dapping tools to shape domes. These steel or wooden tools, which have a rounded end, come in a variety of sizes. The tools create varied domed shapes when hammered into a metal sheet against a dapping die, which has concave depressions of varying sizes to correspond to the different size dapping tools.

Materials. Flat metal discs, dapping tools (die and punch), chasing hammer, solder and soldering tools, file or rough emery paper.

Domes from Discs

A flat disc may be dapped into a dome. The disc can be sawed from a sheet of metal, cut with a disc cutter as described on page 11, or if the metal is thin enough, cut with a shears.

To dome the disc by using a dapping die, place the disc in a large depression and, using a hammer to hit the dapping punch, work down to successively smaller depressions until the desired depth of the dome is achieved (figure 3–12). Using a dapping tool that is slightly smaller than the depression to allow for the thickness of the metal.

When creating a dome from a disc, you must allow for a decrease in the diameter of the dome as it becomes deeper.

The edge of the dome can be flattened by rubbing it across a file or rough emery paper. A totally flat edge makes soldering easy. When soldering a domed disc to a flat sheet of metal (figure 3–13), always drill a hole in an inconspicuous place before you solder to allow trapped gas to escape.

Doming Sheet Metal

It is possible to dap a dome directly into a large sheet of metal by working against a lead block (figure 3–14). The soft lead will contour to the shape of the metal and at the same time give it support as it is domed. If a steel dapping die were used, it would leave indentations in the metal, which would be difficult to remove. After dapping on lead, remove all traces of the lead with steel wool before continuing work. Otherwise, lead will eventually eat holes in the metal.

Making a Bead

To make a hollow bead, solder two domes together (figures 3–15 and 3–16). But before doing this, drill a small hole in the center of

FIG. 3–12   Insert the disc into the dapping die. Form the metal into a dome by hitting the dapping punch with a chasing hammer.

FIG. 3–13   Earrings constructed by soldering domes onto a sheet of metal. The texture was added with a center punch.

FIG. 3–14   Create a dome in the center of a sheet of metal by hammering it with a dapping punch against a lead block.

FIG. 3–15   Melt the solder paillons onto the edge of the dome.

FIG. 3–16   Solder the two domes together after drilling a hole in the domes to allow gas to escape and to permit stringing of the completed bead.

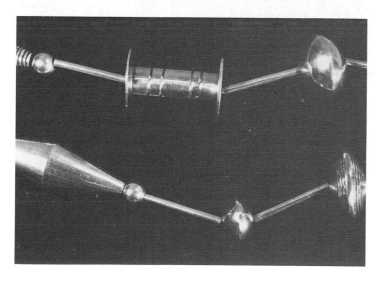

FIG. 3–17   Among the beads on this necklace are two made by soldering two domes together. Other beads were made with tubing, cast forms, and constructed cones.

one of the domes to allow gas to escape when the work is heated. (It is easiest to drill on the concave side of a dome.) Failure to drill this hole will make it impossible to solder the domes together. The hole may also be used for stringing the bead (in which case, both domes must be drilled).

If the bead has been in the pickle, it should be soaked or boiled in a solution of baking soda and water in order to neutralize any acid that is trapped in its hollow. The bead is then filed and polished.

Making Domed Earrings without Soldering

Materials. 24-gauge sheet metal, jump rings, dapping tools, lead block, jeweler's saw, earwires, small shears, a drill with a small bit, filing and polishing tools.

Use 24-gauge sheet metal because of its light weight and the ease with which it is formed. Saw or cut shapes such as rectangles, circles, or triangles for your design. Then with dapping punches, strike the metal against a lead block, impressing a number of

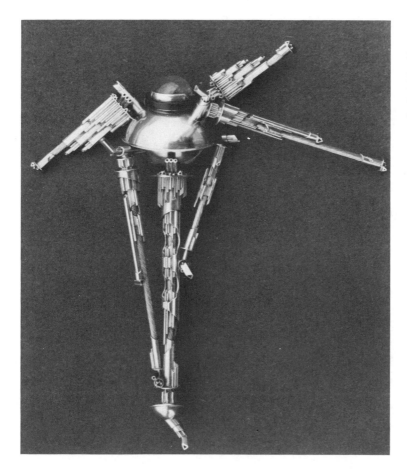

FIG. 3–18 Richard Mawdsley. "Oculi Rectus Superioris #1." Pin of 14K gold, rutilated quartz, and black onyx, including a domed form. *Courtesy of the artist.*

FIG. 3–19 Earrings made by hammering the metal with dapping punches against a lead block.

different size domes into the metal. Drill holes for the links that will connect the parts of the earring and one hole for the earwire. Be careful not to drill the holes too close to the edge of the metal. To finish, file the edges, emery, and polish. Add jump rings and earwires (figure 3–19).

Masonite Die Forming

Masonite die forming involves sinking a piece of sheet metal into a hollow die, which is made by cutting the design out of a block of Masonite-covered plywood (figure 3–20). The plywood gives the die depth, while the Masonite provides the strength necessary for hammering. The shape is cut out and removed, and the sheet metal is then layed over the block and sunk into it with hammers and punches.

This method of forming sheet metal is excellent for making a number of identical forms using a single die. The resulting forms are surrounded by a flange, which can be integrated into the design or cut away. High relief can be achieved because you are sinking against nothing more than air. In general, the possible depth of the sink can be calculated by the formula: depth equals one-half the width of the design. Thus a 3″ (7.5 cm) wide piece can be $1^1/_2$″ (3.8 cm) deep. The wider the design, the deeper the sink can be. A minimum thickness of 22-gauge sheet metal is used in making small forms, and a minimum of 18-gauge is used for larger work.

A vessel can be created by combining two or more forms that have been sunk in the same die (figures 3–21 and 3–22). The two forms are made into mirror images of each other by working from both sides of the die. For a piece such as this, use a band saw to

FIG. 3–20   Masonite die form used to make "Stomach," by Carol Steen. *Courtesy of the artist. Photo by D. James Dee.*

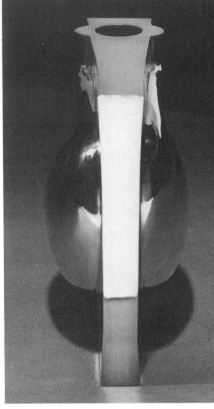

FIG. 3–21   Carol Steen. "Stomach." Side view. Masonite die form in brass. *Courtesy of the artist. Photo by D. James Dee.*

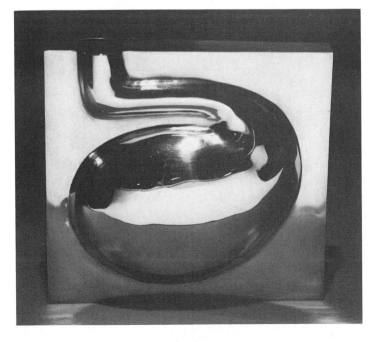

FIG. 3–22   Carol Steen. "Stomach." Front view. *Courtesy of the artist. Photo by D. James Dee.*

cut out the form because it will cut perpendicular to the wood surface. Coping and jig saws have a tendency to cut at an angle. The top and bottom of the die form should be as nearly alike as possible.

The following is the method of making a die-formed piece that is used by jeweler Carol Steen.

Making the Die

To make the die, plywood and $1/4''$-thick (6 mm), tempered Masonite are sandwiched together, with the Masonite covering both the top and bottom of the plywood. The thickness of the plywood is determined by the desired depth of the sink. For large, deep work, a number of pieces of $1/2''$ (1.3 cm) or $3/4''$ (2 cm) plywood can be laminated together. Leave approximately $2''$ (5 cm) of wood surrounding the design to provide a surface to which the metal can be clamped.

The Masonite and plywood are glued together using a generous amount of white glue. The glue should ooze out of the cracks when the wood is pressed together. Clamp the wood together, using C clamps, until the glue is dry. Space the clamps well to maintain even pressure.

When the block is complete, transfer or glue the design onto the Masonite, being certain to center it. The design should be curved rather than angular, for the metal will not conform easily to an angular shape.

The best saw for cutting out your design is a band saw with a $1/2''$ (1.3 cm) blade. Since the band saw uses a continuous-band blade, it cannot be inserted through a hole drilled in the interior of the wood. You will have to begin cutting from the edge and work your way into the interior. If this cut weakens the block, it can be reinforced by gluing a strip of wood onto the side. The die shown in figure 3–20 is reinforced in this manner. This particular die was cut open at the top for a design modification, and wood reinforcements were added to hold the resulting two pieces together.

Since it is difficult and often impossible to cut the entire shape out by simply following the outline, it is best to begin by removing the bulk of the laminated wood and Masonite in sections. First, cut a line up the center of the shape. After backing out of this cut, make several cuts radiating out at angles (figure 3–23). In this way, small sections can be removed until only a small border of excess laminate remains. Now the laminate can be easily cut along the outline.

If a band saw is not available and you must use a jig or coping saw, first drill a hole in the interior of the design to accept the blade. Insert the blade and attach it to the saw. By starting the cut

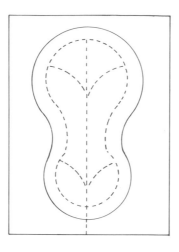

FIG. 3–23   To cut an intricate form out of a laminated block, first cut small sections from the center of the form before trying to cut along the actual form.

within the design, no patching is necessary. While cutting, hold the blade perpendicular to the wood.

After the shape is cut out, file it smooth with a coarse file, such as a half-round or flat Surform file. Be sure to smooth the first ¼″ (6 mm) from the top and bottom of the die. It is this edge to which the metal will conform.

Forming the Metal

Cut the metal sheet, leaving a 1″ (2.5 cm) border around the area to be sunk. This border, called the *flange*, can be made larger if the design calls for it. When sinking, the metal is drawn from the flange, so it will get smaller in places. Anneal the metal and center it carefully over the cutout portion of the die.

Use at least four C clamps of the same size to clamp the metal firmly across the top of the die. (The clamps can also serve as a stand for the die.) If possible, clamp the die to something stationary so that it will not move as work progresses.

Begin by "finding" the edges of the hollow using a rawhide or rubber mallet. Be certain to keep the flange hammered flat against the die during the process. When the shape is visible, use tools such as small mushroom stakes, large dapping punches, and forming hammers to sink the metal further. Work from the edge toward the center, making sure that the edge is well defined before proceeding.

To reach narrow areas or for work on small forms, use smaller tools, such as small dapping punches and chasing tools.

The amount of sink possible at the center of a piece is approximately equal to one-half the width of the piece at that point. Therefore, if the piece is 2″ (5 cm) wide, the maximum sink is 1″ (2.5 cm) at its center.

Eventually, the metal will become work-hardened. To prevent it from cracking, unclamp and anneal it. Then reclamp it onto the die and continue working until you achieve a deeper, more refined shape. Repeat this process at least three or more times. The surface should be relatively smooth at this point.

Planishing

To further refine the form, remove it from the die and planish over stakes (polished metal forms for shaping metal) or dapping punches with a planishing hammer (figure 3–4). Planishing toughens and finishes the metal by removing coarser hammer blows. The metal is hammered against the form until it assumes the desired shape. When planishing, work from the center toward the edge. (This is the opposite of the direction of working when the metal is in the die). If you are hammering correctly, the hammering will produce a ringing rather than a hollow sound.

Be sure to keep the contact surfaces of the stakes and hammer highly polished. Any scratches or dents will be transferred to the metal. To remove dents in the stake and hammer surfaces, file and emery, using successively finer emery until you get to 600 grit. Then polish by machine with stainless-steel polish.

Planishing leaves a series of small hammer marks in a regular pattern over the surface of the metal. This can be left as the final finish, or it can be filed, emeried, and polished to a completely smooth finish.

Using the Form

The resulting form may be cut out with a jeweler's saw and soldered onto a flat piece of metal. (Drill a small hole to allow gas to escape during soldering.)

Two forms made by working from the top and bottom of the die can be combined in a single piece. In this case, plan to include the flange as part of the design. Rarely can two forms be cut out without a flange and fit together exactly, since they have only the thickness of the metal edges for a soldering surface. If the shapes are even slightly different, the two forms will not meet and soldering will be impossible.

The work "Stomach" (figures 3–21 and 3–22) was constructed by soldering two identical die forms perpendicular to a strip of sheet metal. One form was soldered on each side of the metal strip with medium wire solder. Extra metal ($\frac{1}{8}''$ [3 mm] per side) was left overlapping the seam to provide a shelf onto which the solder was fed. This overlap was later cut off and filed flush, leaving crisp edges and an imperceptible seam.

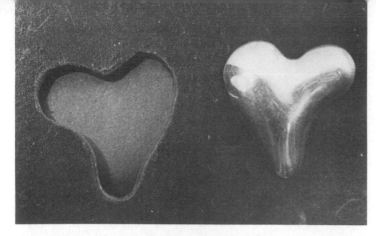

FIG. 3–24 Miniature Masonite die with metal form that was made from it.

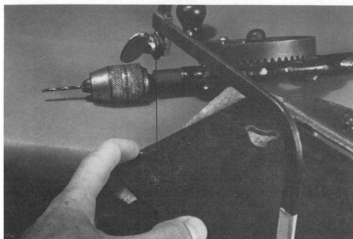

FIG. 3–25 To make a miniature Masonite die, insert the jeweler's saw blade into a drilled hole and saw out the desired form.

FIG. 3–26 File the form with a needle file.

FIG. 3–27 Anneal the metal before sinking it into the die.

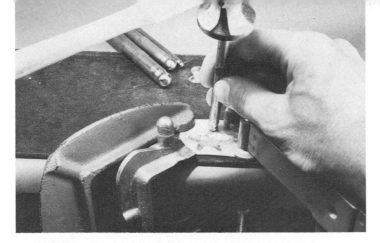

FIG. 3–28 Clamp the metal onto the die and sink it into the form with dapping punches. Anneal when necessary.

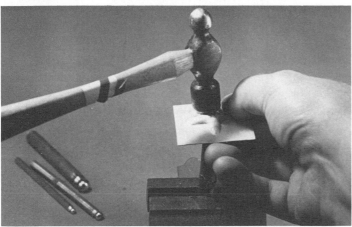

FIG. 3–29 Planish the metal over stakes or dapping punches.

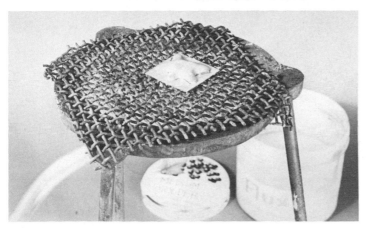

FIG. 3–30 Solder the die-formed shape onto a backing. Heat mainly from below.

FIG. 3–31 Completed die-formed cufflinks.

After soldering, the entire piece was filed, emeried, and polished.

Miniature Masonite Die Forms

For small jewelry, tiny dies can be made by cutting shapes out of ¼″ (6 mm) tempered Masonite with a jeweler's saw. No plywood is necessary. Note that the thin Masonite limits these forms to a maximum depth of sink of ³/₁₆″ (5 mm). For this purpose, 22-gauge sheet metal is excellent. The procedure for cutting a miniature die and forming the metal is outlined in figures 3–24 through 3–31.

Repoussé and Chasing

A highly controlled method of forming sheet metal, with great possibilities for sculptural form, is accomplished by using a combination of repoussé and chasing (figures 3–32 and 3–33). Either process is also effective when used independently. Repoussé work

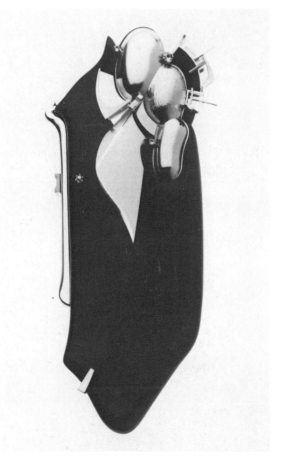

FIG. 3–32   Jem Freyaldenhoven. "Krasnaya." Wall hanging of sterling silver, 14K gold, pearl, and acrylic. Chasing, repoussé, construction, and plastic lamination. *Courtesy of the artist.*

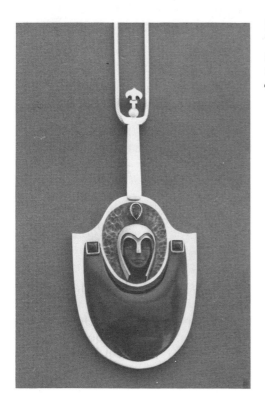

FIG. 3–33   Gene and Hiroko Pijanowski. "Gladiator." Pendant of silver, gold, copper, ruby, garnets, Shakudo (Japanese alloy). Constructed, repoussé, and chased on the face. *Courtesy of the artists.*

FIG. 3–34   Marcia Lewis. "Angel Gabriel." Neckpiece of sterling silver. Metal is chased, split, and forged. *Courtesy of the artist. Photo by Werner Kalber.*

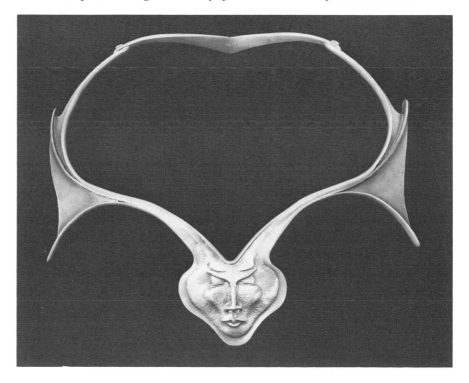

is done by hammering the metal from the back, creating a relief on the front of the metal sheet. Chasing is done from the front, creating a depression in the front of the metal. In both cases, punches are struck against the metal, causing it to stretch.

Materials.   Annealed sheet metal (no thinner than 22-gauge), dapping punches, chasing tools, chasing hammer, scribes, pitch bowl (or sandbag or lead block), torch, pickling and polishing equipment, tweezers or pliers, planishing hammer, jeweler's saw.

Begin by experimenting with different dapping punches and chasing tools to achieve variety in depth, sharp and soft edges, and narrow and wide forms.

The gauge of the metal is chosen to accommodate the size and depth of the design. The deeper the form, the thicker the metal must be to allow for greater stretching. A large work would be made from 18-gauge sheet metal to provide strength.

Transfer your design to the back side of the metal. Use a scribe to make the lines more permanent. The sheet should be larger than the design so that it can be held by the pitch and not interfere with the form.

Supporting the Work

The metal can be supported on a sandbag or lead block. If lead is used, remove all traces of it with steel wool before continuing. Pitch, however, is the most effective, though messy, means of securing the metal.

Pitch is made from a mixture of 6 parts Burgundy pitch, 8 parts plaster of paris, and 1 part tallow or linseed oil. Jeweler's pitch may also be purchased, ready mixed, from a jewelry supply house. Greater amounts of tallow or oil may be added in cool weather, when the pitch is too hard and brittle.

The pitch is held in a container that will not break from the impact of hammering. A heavy, round-bottomed iron bowl set into a leather, rubber, or wooden ring allows you to set the work at the most convenient angle (see figure 3–36).

Heat the pitch by brushing a soft flame back and forth over the surface. Moving the flame will prevent the heat from becoming too concentrated. Be careful not to burn the pitch. If you see smoke, you are using too much heat. Overheated pitch can explode and cause severe burns.

When the pitch is soft, place the annealed metal on it, sinking it until it is held firmly in place. The corners of the metal can be bent down to provide added security. One corner can be bent upward so that the metal can be easily removed after working. Some pitch should flow over the edges. If the metal does not sink sufficiently into the pitch, the metal can be heated until the pitch below it becomes soft. Then the metal is pressed down and sunk further.

The pitch is left to air cool or run under cool water to hasten the cooling process.

Forming the Metal

To form the metal, begin by using large dapping punches or the rounded end of a hammer to punch out the general form. For small work, use small dapping punches and rounded chasing tools. A chasing hammer is preferable to a regular household hammer for striking punches because its wide face provides a larger area for hitting. Punches are held in the weaker hand and hit directly downward, with the hammer held in the stronger hand. At this stage, the form will look quite crude.

Do not try to stretch the metal all at once or it will crack. It must be gradually coaxed from one place to another and then annealed whenever the metal becomes work-hardened.

After the basic form has been punched out, the metal is removed from the pitch by heating it with a torch until it can be easily pried out with a pick, tweezers, or pliers. It is then annealed and cleaned. To clean, plunge the hot, annealed metal into water. Most of the pitch will flake off, and the remaining pitch can be removed by heating with a torch until it turns to gray ash, which is then brushed off. Turpentine, alcohol, or benzine (not to be confused with benzene, or benzol, which is highly toxic) will also remove pitch. (Good ventilation is important when using any cleaning solvent.) A cloth dipped in melted paraffin and wiped over the warmed metal will also aid in removing the pitch.

The annealed and cleaned metal is now returned to the pitch to be chased on the opposite side. Using a scrap of sheet metal, make a mound of soft pitch in the center of the pitch bowl and place the metal over it so that the hollow created by the repoussé work is filled. (To chase a three-dimensional form such as a cylinder, fill the cylinder with pitch.)

The chasing tools (figure 3–35) are now used to refine the raised form. A good variety of differently shaped chasing tools will allow you to shape specific areas. These tools can be readily purchased, or made, if you wish, from tool steel. Chasing tools are held at an angle and hammered toward you (figure 3–36). This gives greater control by enabling you to see what you are doing. The tool is moved along by the blow of the hammer.

Continue the process of repoussé and chasing until the form is well defined. When completed, the form can be further smoothed by planishing the metal over small stakes or dapping tools held in place by a vise, as shown in figure 3–29. A hammer may be held in a vise and used as a stake.

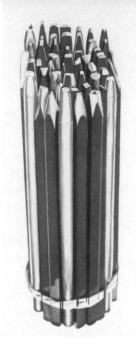

FIG. 3–35   Chasing tools.
*Courtesy of William Dixon
Company.*

FIG. 3–36   To chase a line, work toward you and
move the chasing tool along by hitting it with the
chasing hammer.

Finishing the Piece

The piece can be filed and emeried if a completely smooth surface
is desired. However, care must be taken not to go through the metal,
which has already been thinned by the repoussé and chasing
processes. If necessary, a small crack can be filled using solder of
the appropriate color. However, solder is rarely the exact color of
the metal and should be avoided when possible.

The finished form can be left as a relief portion of a flat sheet or
cut from its background using a jeweler's saw. A cutout form can
then be soldered onto a backing of sheet metal. (Remember to drill
a minute hole for air to escape when the piece is heated during
soldering.)

Sculptural Form: Casting

4

Casting jewelry involves pouring molten metal into a mold which has itself been cast from a model, carved, or pressed. This mold may be made from a variety of materials including cuttlebone, plaster, charcoal, clay, sand, or investment, a heat-resistant plaster compound. There are a number of casting methods in which the metal enters the mold by force of gravity, steam, air pressure, vacuum suction or centrifugal force. The process can be executed using simple, inexpensive materials or highly developed and expensive equipment.

Casting is a unique process in jewelry making and presents wide possibilities for sculptural form. The model is usually made in wax and can therefore be sculpted into any shape, be it figurative or abstract. Wax offers little resistance to pressure and can be modeled in great detail. Only in wax is it possible to achieve such great variation in texture and three-dimensional form. In designing for a cast piece, it is important to appreciate these specific qualities of the medium and how it differs from working directly in metal. Taking a design that can easily be constructed and trying to cast it will result in work that looks imitative. Such a piece would not have the integrity of work designed specifically with the casting process in mind.

Cuttlebone Casting

Materials. Cuttlebone, jeweler's saw, sandpaper, carving tools, objects to be pressed into the cuttlebone, toothpick, 14-gauge wire or a matchstick, wire brush, binding wire, pliers, charcoal

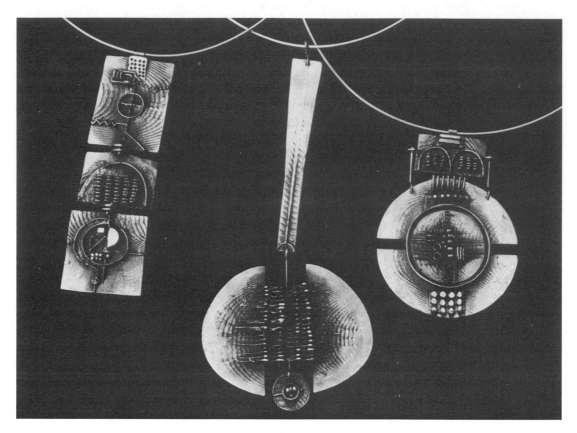

FIG. 4–1 Bob Natalini. Pendants, cast in cuttlebone. *Courtesy of the artist.*

block, files, tongs, torch with a large tip, flux (borax), casting metal (sterling silver, brass, bronze, or gold), water and detergent.

One direct method of casting is done using a cuttlebone mold. Large pieces of cuttlebone may be purchased at a jewelry supply house. This soft material may be carved or used to take an impression of a small, rigid model. The casting is done using gravity to draw the molten metal into the mold cavity.

For use in casting, the top and bottom of the cuttlebone are sawed off flat for stability, and to provide a surface in which to carve an entry channel for the metal. The cuttlebone is sawed lengthwise in half with a jeweler's saw (figure 4–2) and the inner, soft sides sanded flat on a piece of sandpaper taped to a flat surface (figure 4–3).

Making the Impression

The design to be cast may be carved directly into the cuttlebone, or an impression can be made from objects such as jewelry, coins, small toy parts, knives, and other tools. When an impression is

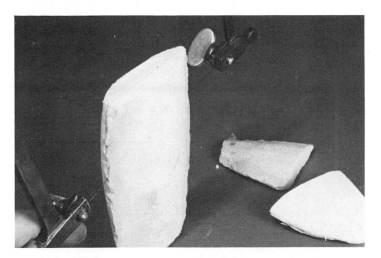

FIG. 4–2 Saw the cuttlebone in half after sawing off the two ends.

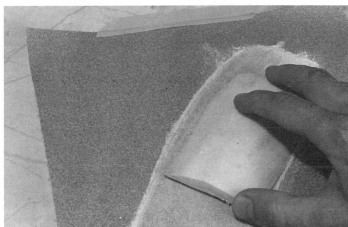

FIG. 4–3 Sand the inside surface of the cuttlebone flat.

FIG. 4–4 Different tools and objects can be used to make an impression in the cuttlebone.

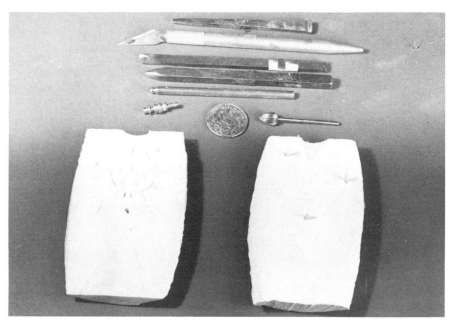

made from a complex form, however, some of the details may be lost as the model is removed from the cuttlebone.

An impression of a three-dimensional model such as a coin may be made in the round by first pressing the model halfway into one of the halves of the cuttlebone. Then place three or four short pegs made from a toothpick, wire, or wooden matchstick around the model so that they will extend into the other half of the cuttlebone. Now carefully press the two halves together. After the impression is taken, separate the halves and carefully remove the model.

The characteristic rippled texture of cuttlebone castings can be accentuated by rubbing the inner surface of the cuttlebone with a wire brush after the impression has been taken. The softer bone will powder off leaving the denser, patterned grain.

Completing the Mold and Crucible

Carve a channel leading to the top of the mold into both halves and a funnel in the top of the channel to act as a receptacle for the molten metal. Small air vents can be carved radiating out from the impression to allow gasses to escape when casting. These vents should not pierce the cuttlebone to the outside.

Rejoin the two halves of the cuttlebone using the pegs as a key for registration. Bind the halves together using two pieces of binding wire. Use a pair of pliers to make a half twist in a few places to tighten the wire.

A crucible is a heat-resistant container for melting metal. To make a crucible for cuttlebone casting, carve a depression in a charcoal block. File the block to fit the contour of the cuttlebone and bind them together with binding wire (figure 4–5). Carve a channel from the depression to the funnel in the cuttlebone.

Casting the Piece

Now you are ready to cast your piece. Stand the mold on end, propped upright between two bricks. Heat the metal in the crucible using a torch (figure 4–6). Determining how much metal to use is usually a matter of guesswork. Of course, it is better to err by using too much than to be caught short. When the metal has melted, add a pinch of flux (borax) to aid in the flow of the metal.

When the metal is molten, *immediately* tip the crucible-mold using the tongs. The metal will flow into the mold. When the metal has cooled, remove the casting. Saw off extra metal with a jeweler's saw and file smooth. Polish the piece using a brass brush, water and detergent.

The cuttlebone mold can usually be used only one time. The charcoal crucible can be used until it breaks.

FIG. 4–5   Fasten the cuttlebone to the charcoal crucible with binding wire.

FIG. 4–6   Melt the metal in the charcoal crucible and pour it into the cuttlebone mold.

FIG. 4–7   Completed pendant, cast in cuttlebone.

Charcoal Casting

Materials. Two flat blocks of charcoal, a carving knife or other carving tool, sandpaper, binding wire, pliers, crucible with a handle, flux (borax), casting metal, torch with a large tip, jeweler's saw, files, polishing materials.

Charcoal casting is one of the simplest methods of casting. The design is carved directly into the charcoal, and the casting is accomplished by the force of gravity. Therefore no elaborate equipment is needed.

Two pieces of charcoal block are needed to form the mold. Charcoal blocks can be purchased at a jewelry supply store. Sand both blocks smooth with sandpaper that has been taped to a flat surface to make it flat and rigid. Carve the design into one of the blocks using a small knife or pointed tool.

Next, carve a channel running from the design to the top of the block. At the top of the channel carve a funnel to accept the molten metal. A half-funnel shape is also carved at the top of the second charcoal block. The rest of the second block is left uncarved in order to create a flat back for the cast piece. Bind the two blocks together with two pieces of binding wire. Twist a kink in several places in the wires using a pair of pliers to bring the blocks into close contact.

Heat the metal in a crucible with a torch. For charcoal casting, a small crucible with a handle may be purchased at a jewelry supply store. Add a pinch of flux (borax) to aid in the flow of the metal. Rest the mold on a heat-resistant surface, and pour the molten metal into the mold. When it cools, remove the cast metal.

Extra metal is sawed off using a jeweler's saw and then the casting is filed. Clean the piece with a brass brush dipped in water and detergent. This brushing will leave a polished surface on the metal. The cast piece may also be polished by hand or machine.

Making a Wax Model: Lost Wax Casting

Lost wax casting is another method of making a mold into which molten metal is poured to create the finished piece. The model is made in wax, cast in investment, and melted out of the mold in a furnace. The cavity is then filled with molten metal. The process thus proceeds from a wax positive to a negative form cast in investment and lastly to a metal positive. It is an involved process, but it allows for the casting of intricate and exact replicas.

Remember that your metal jewelry will weigh many times the weight of the wax model. This change in weight varies with the type of metal used. Using too much wax is a common mistake made by the novice, and many first pieces are extraordinarily heavy.

FIG. 4–8 Jaclyn Davidson. "Group Identification." Bracelet of sterling, cast in two pieces and soldered together. *Courtesy of the artist. Photo by J. David Long.*

Waxes

Wax is available in a variety of shapes and hardnesses. It can be purchased in sheet, tube, rod, wire and block form to suit the shape and size of the design that you wish to execute. Wax size is measured in terms of dimension, weight, or gauge. The higher the gauge, the thinner the wax. Different hardnesses are available for variation in strength, flexibility, and ease with which it can be dripped, filed, folded, pulled and pressed. Soft wax, for example, can be directly modeled with your hands. The hard waxes can be drilled, filed, and carved. Different waxes can be worked in combination with each other.

Scrap wax and wax filings may be saved and formed into blocks or sheets for future use. Scraps of different hardnesses may be combined. Aluminum foil folded into a pan shape is excellent for forming recycled wax. To make a wax sheet, use a flat pan into which 1 inch of water has been poured. Pour the melted wax slowly into the pan. The wax will float on the surface of the water and form a sheet when hardened. To free the sheet from the pan, cut around the edge using a knife or razor.

Caution: Wax is explosive when overheated. Heat wax in a double boiler to avoid contact with the heating elements. Coffee cans and old pots are useful for this purpose. *Never allow the wax to smoke.*

Wax Tools

Wax can be cut with a scissors or razor, or sawed using a special wax blade in your saw frame. Hand files, knives or different burs in the flexible shaft can be used to shape the wax (figure 4–9). A half-round file is used to shape curved forms such as the inside of a ring band. Rough files will not clog as easily as fine files and are therefore more suited to sculpting wax. To clean the file, heat it to melt the wax and wipe with a paper towel.

Many tools for modeling wax can be improvised from things found around the home or studio. Scratch pens, tweezers, discarded dental tools, nut picks, and thin knives are all handy for creating different effects with wax. A set of tools can even be fashioned from several pieces of coat hanger wire hammered and filed at one end into different shapes.

Heating Wax

Not all waxes need to be heated in order to be modeled. However, many effects can only be achieved by heating. Sheet wax, for example, can be softened by dipping it into warm water and is excellent for taking impressions of textured surfaces (figure 4–10). When taking impressions, oil may be used to lubricate the object, making removal of the wax easier. In its softened state, sheet wax can also be folded or stretched into three-dimensional forms. For other effects, greater, more concentrated heat than warm water is needed. A bunsen burner, alcohol lamp, or, when these are not available, a candle, are good sources of heat. A candle, however, will deposit carbon on the model which may cause some problems in casting. Alcohol lamps and wicks may be purchased at a jewelry supply store. An alcohol lamp can also be made using a small covered jar with a hole pierced through the metal cover to accommodate a wick. Use only denatured alcohol for fuel in an alcohol lamp.

Techniques for Working in Wax

There are numerous techniques for working in wax, many of which can be discovered through experimentation. When using any new material, it takes time to get a feel for its qualities.

Tools to mold and join wax can be heated and used either directly on the wax model to fuse, or to add melted wax for joining or building up surfaces. To attach wax to wax, heat a pointed tool and seal the joint where they meet (figure 4–12). Gaps may be filled using a spatula loaded with melted wax and applying it where needed. Be sure to use enough wax to make a strong connection. Excess wax can be removed by scraping and filing.

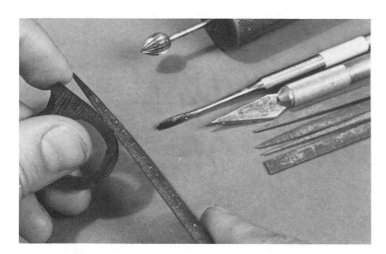

FIG. 4–9   Shape the wax using various tools such as a wax file, dental tools, knives, files, and burs.

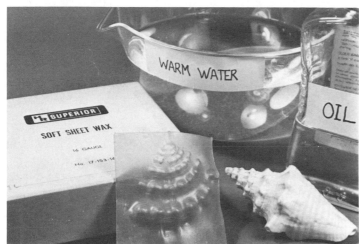

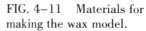

FIG. 4–10   An impression can be taken by heating sheet wax in warm water and pressing the wax over the oiled object.

FIG. 4–11   Materials for making the wax model.

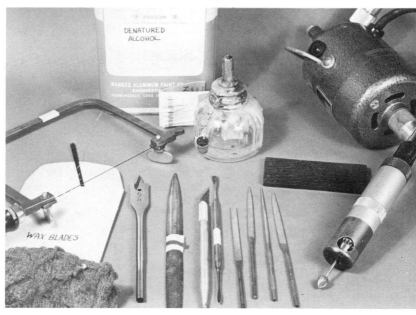

FIG. 4–12 Join wax to wax
with melted wax carried on a
dental tool.

Tools can also be used cold or warmed to scratch or press texture
into the wax. Holes can be pierced in the wax using a heated pin
tool (figure 4–14). The melted wax is then blown out of the hole.
Heat rough edges by running them quickly through the flame to give
them a smooth, finished look.

Another method of using wax for modeling is by dripping it onto a
lubricated surface and building up a form gradually. Oil is a good
lubricant to use so that the wax model can be easily removed when
completed. Thin plastic wrap placed over the surface is also useful
in ensuring easy removal of the wax.

Interesting textures can be created by pouring melted wax into a
jar of cold water or by pouring the wax over snow or ice. Wax

FIG. 4–13 Jaclyn Davidson. "Queen, King, Bishop." A wearable chess set of
sterling silver. Cast in two, three, and four pieces and soldered together. *Courtesy
of the artist. Photo by J. David Long.*

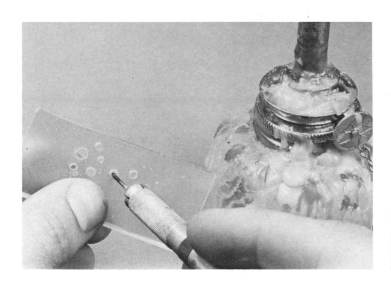

FIG. 4–14   Holes may be poked into the wax with a heated tool. The melted wax is then blown out of the hole.

models may also be cast in molds made out of such materials as plasticene, lead, Styrofoam, or rubber.

To type a word or message onto wax, wrap a warmed sheet of pink wax in plastic wrap and place it in the typewriter. Remove the ribbon and type directly on the plastic wrap. Letters can also be impressed in the wax using rubber printing sets available in stationery and toy stores.

Some stones such as diamonds, saphires, rubies, emeralds, yellow topaz and synthetic stones can be "set" directly in the wax and left intact during casting. Small metal additions such as bezels or metal tubing for tube settings, may also be cast directly in the wax. The molten metal being cast is not hot enough to melt the cold metal. For other stones, a bezel or prong setting may be constructed out of wax to fit the stone perfectly. The stone is carefully removed before casting and the wax prongs or bezel left open, ready to receive the stone after casting. After the piece is cast and polished, the stone is inserted and the prongs or bezel is pushed over the stone to set it in place.

Forming Rings

Wax models for cast rings can be made using file-a-wax cut to the desired thickness. The wax may be cut from a block using a spiral wax blade, or purchased in the correct gauge. To make the ring band, drill a hole in the wax that is slightly smaller than the ring size desired. A ½″ (1.3 cm) drill bit is the average size used for a woman's ring. Later this can be filed to the correct size or drawn down a heated metal ring mandrel to the correct size.

To determine the correct ring size, use a ring sizer or a ring fitting the person for whom it is to be made. Size your model to

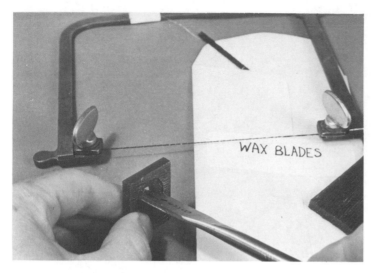

FIG. 4–15 Saw a slab of wax and drill a hole slightly smaller than the desired ring size.

FIG. 4–16 Refine the wax model with steel wool.

allow for filing and polishing. Virtually no shrinkage will take place in the casting. Wide band rings should be made slightly larger to allow for hand swelling and contraction in different temperatures.

Now you are ready to carve the ring, limited in design only by function and comfort.

Wax models for rings can also be drip-formed. To make a mandrel on which to drip a ring form, wrap a 3″ (7.5 cm) piece of ½″ (1.3 cm) diameter dowel with masking tape to create the correct ring size.

Refining and Repairing the Model

Fine files and fine steel wool can be used to refine the surface of the wax model (Figure 4–16). A high polish can be achieved on the wax model by rubbing it with a leather chamois or with a piece of denim cloth to which some paint thinner has been added. Refine the surface of the wax model as much as possible for it is easier to work in the wax than in the cast metal piece.

To repair a broken section of the wax or to fill a gap, melted wax can be added using a dental tool. Pieces of wax may also be joined with a heated tool.

Pressing Soft Sheet Wax into a Plaster Mold

Taking a wax impression from a plaster mold is an excellent means of duplicating a form for casting. The original impression is made by pouring the plaster into a box and laying the object you wish to duplicate into the soft plaster. This object should not have undercuts. Undercuts will make it difficult, if not impossible, to remove the model and the wax from the hardened plaster mold.

The original model may be a found object or may be sculpted from plasticene. Before casting the model in plaster, lubricate it with petroleum jelly for easy removal after the mold has set. It is not necessary to lubricate plasticene because it is oily and will not stick to plaster.

The plaster is mixed in a flexible bowl by *adding the plaster to the water.* Do not add water to the plaster. You will know that you have added enough plaster when it no longer sinks into the water. Use your hand to mix the plaster and water, being certain to remove all lumps. Do not add water or plaster after you have begun mixing. You will notice that heat is generated as the plaster begins to set. Because the plaster begins to set as soon as it is mixed with water, work must proceed quickly.

When the plaster is thoroughly mixed, pour it into a cardboard box or milk container which has been cut open on one side. Allow the plaster to set to the point at which it will support the model. At this point the plaster will be the consistency of sour cream Next, press the model partially into the plaster so that it may be lifted out easily after the plaster sets. Allow the plaster to set and dry for several hours before removing the model. Now you have a plaster mold into which you can press sheet wax.

The wax may be softened in warm water and pressed into the mold, or else a layer of wax may be dripped over the mold. After the wax has cooled, it is lifted from the mold, trimmed and cast in metal.

Measuring the Metal

When the wax model is complete, it can be measured or weighed in order to determine the amount of metal that will be needed for casting.

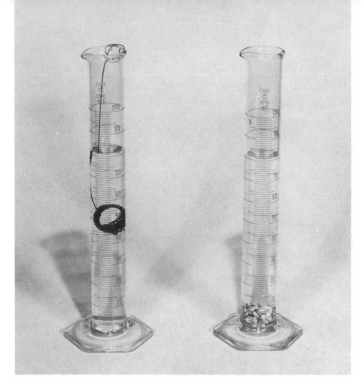

FIG. 4–17   Water displacement method of determining the amount of metal needed for casting. *Courtesy of Kerr Manufacturing Co.*

FIG. 4–18   Gram scale. *Courtesy of Allcraft.*

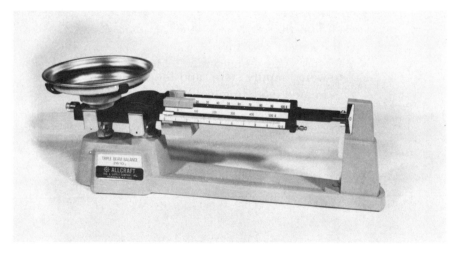

One method of measuring is by water displacement. The model is immersed in a partially filled, graduated cylinder. The model is kept from floating by a thin wire wrapped carefully around it (see figure 4–17). The new water level is noted. The model is then removed and casting metal is added to the cylinder until the water reaches the same level as it reached when the model was submerged. An additional few grams of metal should be added to allow for sprues and a small reservoir of metal needed during casting.

Another method of determining the amount of metal needed for casting is by weighing the model using a gram scale (figure 4–18), and multiplying this weight by the specific gravity of the metal you wish to use for casting (see page 209). Add an additional few grams for a button and sprues.

Making an Investment Mold

Investment is a porous, heat-resistant, plaster-like material used to make molds for lost-wax casting. It is capable of reproducing fine detail and withstands the heat of the burnout and casting processes. Plaster of paris is not a substitute for investment.

The first step in making the mold is to sprue and mount the wax model so the investment can be poured around it.

Spruing

Materials. Round wax sprue wire, alcohol lamp, wax tools, the wax model.

Sprues are round wax wires which are attached to the wax model. When burned out, they leave channels through which the molten metal travels to the casting. These channels also allow wax to escape in burnout. In addition, the sprues support the model in the investing (mold-making) process. Wax sprue wire is purchased in a jewelry supply store, and the sprues are attached to the model using a heated modeling tool.

A wax model must be correctly sprued in order for the molten metal to reach all parts of the casting as quickly as possible, before the metal freezes. For this reason, the positioning of sprues is important. Sprues must be short, direct, and smooth to allow for smooth flow of molten metal. The sprue should be placed in the least obtrusive area to avoid interference with details that will be difficult to restore when the sprues are removed after casting. Because it is difficult to get saws and files into concave areas, attach the sprue to a convex form when possible.

Sprue to the heaviest area, and make the sprue thick enough so that the metal will not freeze in the sprue channel before it has a chance to fill the model cavity.

If more than one sprue is needed, auxiliary sprues should terminate in one main sprue which will later be attached to the sprue base. Any low point in your model should get an auxilliary sprue so that the entering metal always flows in the same direction and does not have to flow in the opposite direction to reach parts of the mold.

Whenever the metal is forced from a large section into a thinner section and then on to a thicker section, a sprue should be added to the thick section after the constriction. If this is not done, the metal may freeze before it flows through the constriction and an incomplete casting will result.

When attaching a sprue to a flat sheet of wax, it is advisable to position the sheet at an angle rather than parallel to the base. In this position, the molten metal entering at a rapid speed will not splash back on itself when it hits the wall of the cavity and impede the flow of the metal throughout the mold.

The number and placement of the sprues is dependent upon the size and design of the piece to be cast. A small simple piece may require only one sprue. A complex or large piece will require more. There is no precise rule to follow for spruing because every piece is different and therefore requires a different arrangement. The principle is to sprue the model so that the metal will flow smoothly and quickly to all sections of the mold.

FIG. 4–19 Attach the model to the sprue base with wax heated by an alcohol lamp.

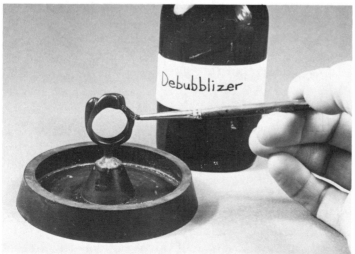

FIG. 4–20 Coat the model and sprues with debubblizer.

Mounting the Sprued Model

Materials. Rubber or metal sprue base (or a sheet of glass, rubber, or metal), plasticene, soft wax, debubblizer (or tincture of green soap or denatured alcohol), small brush, a stainless steel investment flask (or tin can opened on both ends).

After the model has been sprued, it is ready to be mounted on the sprue base. The sprue base will support the model while you are pouring on the investment, and it forms a funnel shape in the mold for the molten metal to pass through. A sprue base can be purchased, or one can be made by modeling a smooth cone of plasticene about 1″ (2.5 cm) in diameter on a metal, glass, or rubber sheet.

The sprue is attached to the sprue base with wax (figure 4–19). Add enough wax so that the sprue flares slightly at this juncture rather than thinning. If this joint is thinner than the sprue, the flow of molten metal during casting will be impeded and an incomplete casting will result.

Using a fine brush, coat the model and sprues with a layer of debubblizer, tincture of green soap, or denatured alcohol (figure 4–20). This coating will break the surface tension on the wax and allow the investment to flow easily over the model. In this way, any detail on the model will be preserved. Let the debubblizer dry.

Next, a purchased stainless steel investment flask, or a tin can opened on both ends, is placed over the model and attached to the base using plasticene or soft wax. The flask should extend above the model at least ½″ (1.3 cm).

Investing

Materials. Water, flexible rubber bowl, investment, spatula, spoon, vibrator, small brush, small knife.

To mix the investment, put water in a rubber mixing bowl. The water should be enough to fill approximately two-thirds of the investment flask. Add the investment to the water by sprinkling it in until it no longer sinks into the water. (The investment may also be mixed by weight. A ratio of approximately 40 parts water to 100 parts powder is recommended by most manufacturers.) Mix with a spatula, or on a vibrator, which will help eliminate unwanted air bubbles. (A vibrator for this purpose may be purchased at a jewelry supply store.) The investment should form a creamy smooth paste when mixed. (Note specific directions on investment packaging.) Mixing must be done quickly before the investment sets.

After the investment is mixed, it is poured into the flask. To insure reproduction of finer details, initial coats of investmemt may be brushed on and gently blown by mouth onto the wax model.

FIG. 4–21   Hold the flask at an angle while pouring the investment. A vibrator is used to remove air bubbles. *Courtesy of Kerr Manufacturing Co.*

When pouring the investment, tilt the flask at an angle to prevent air from being trapped in the mold (figure 4–21). Do not pour directly onto the wax model. A spoon may be used to direct the investment and to break the fall.

While the investment is being poured, the flask should be placed on a vibrator to remove any air bubbles. Failure to remove air bubbles will result in a coating of small granules on the surface of the casting. If a vibrator is not available, knock gently on the work table using your hand or a mallet.

Fill the flask completely. A slight overflow may be scraped level using a knife once the investment has set. Figure 4–22 shows the wax model in place on the sprue base, surrounded by the flask and investment.

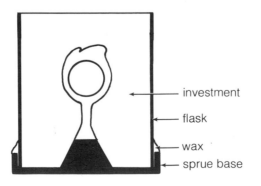

FIG. 4–22   Invested flask for centrifugal casting.

investment

flask

wax

sprue base

Jean Battles-Irvin. Necklace. Mixed media.

Barbara Mail. "Shades of Scarlet." Picture frame of ivory, 14K gold, silver, copper, tintype, peridot, electroformed tulip petal.

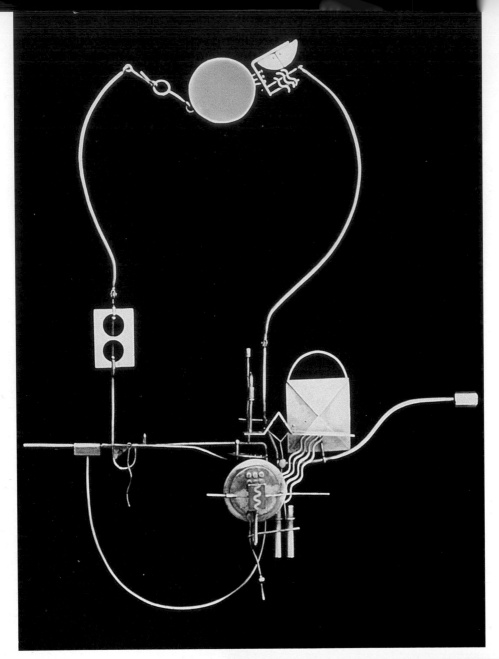

Bob Natalini. Necklace of silver,
14K gold, copper, turquoise, rose
quartz. 1972.

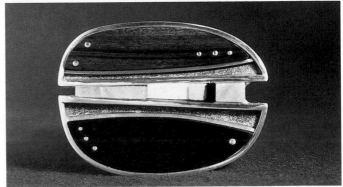

Donna Matles. Buckle of ebony,
ironwood, shell, turquoise, buffalo
horn, sterling silver. *Photo by the
artist*.

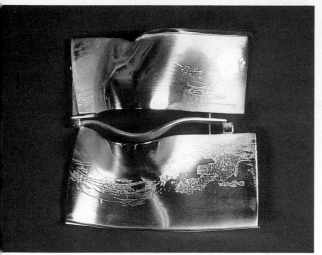

Adine Kaufman. Pin of etched silver.

Elizabeth Weeden. Neckpiece of coiled silver
wire, mallard feathers. *Photo by R. A. Lafande.*

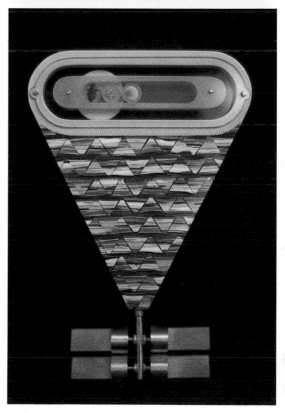

Bob Natalini. Brooch of 18K gold, polyester,
natural objects. 1974.

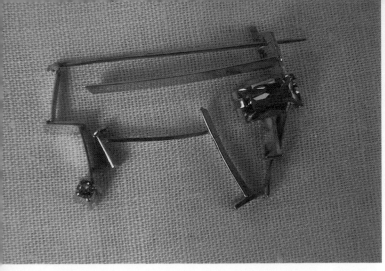

Adine Kaufman. Pin of silver, 14K gold, aquamarine.

Tom Farrell. Pin of silver, copper, and tintype, with line inlay. *Photo by Vincent Pidone.*

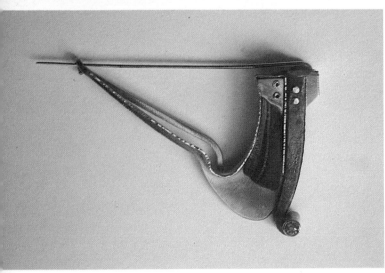

Barbara Mail. "Shooting Stars Revisited." Pin of abalone shell, hand-made nail, 14K gold, silver, aquamarine.

Jean Battles-Irvin. Necklace. Mixed media and fiber techniques.

Judy Moonelis. Necklace of stoneware, porcelain, sequins.

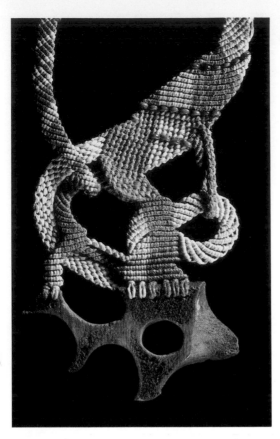

Gammy Miller. Neckpiece of soupbone, fiber. *Photo by Ken Kimerling*.

Enid Kaplan. Bangle bracelet of 14K red, yellow, white gold; silver; brass; copper; citrines; ebony.

Enid Kaplan. Comb of silver, copper, nickel, brass, carnelian, acrylic.

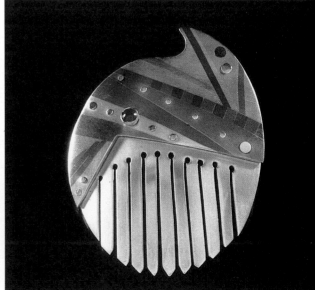

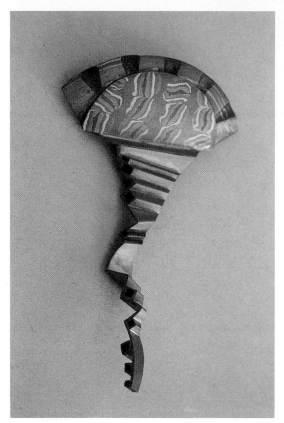

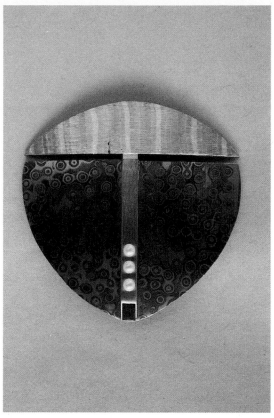

Chuck Evans. Brooch of combined metals.

Chuck Evans. Brooch of Mokume, lamination, cultured pearls.

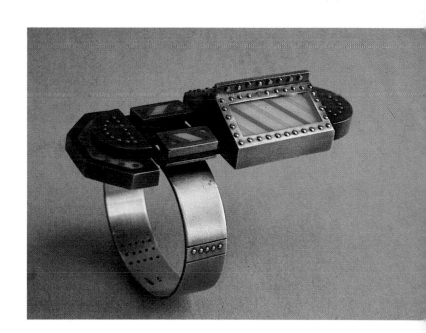

Richard Helzer. Bracelet of acrylic
(laminated and inlaid), metals.

Gayle Saunders. Necklace of sterling silver, 14K green and pink gold, 18K yellow gold, mother of pearl beads.

Ronna Silver. "Waterfall Brooch #2." Silver, citrine. 1979. *Photo by the artist.*

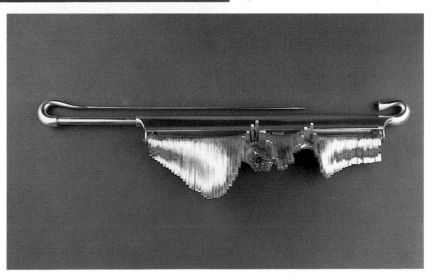

The investment will set in about 15 minutes. After about one-half hour, carefully remove the sprue base. The conical cavity created by the base will hold a reservoir of molten metal, called a button, that will feed the casting as it cools and shrinks. Because it is so thick, the button remains molten after the rest of the casting has begun to solidify.

Before the mold is ready for burnout, it must dry for approximately an hour, but it must not be allowed to dry out completely before placing it in the burnout furnace. A dry mold will crack during burnout. If burnout must be delayed, place the flask in a tightly sealed plastic bag to keep it moist.

Burnout in an Electric Furnace

Materials. Furnace, casting tongs, wire mesh.

The purpose of burnout is to eliminate the wax or other model material (such as casting plastic or found objects) as well as the moisture in the investment. In the process of burning out, the investment is also heated to the proper temperature for casting.

Burnout furnaces may be either gas or electric. Electric furnaces are used by most schools and craftspeople. Gas furnaces are most often used for production casting. A pyrometer on the outside of the furnace indicates the temperature within. Furnaces can be purchased at a jewelry supply store.

Electric enameling kilns are sometimes converted for use in wax elimination. However, the exposure of the kiln elements to wax and water vapor will shorten the life of the kiln. If there is no vent at the top of the kiln to allow for gases to escape, the door to the kiln should be left open a crack while the kiln is on.

With any kiln, proper ventilation (an exhaust hood) is essential to remove the fumes created in the burnout process. Some of the wax can be removed before it vaporizes by placing the flask on a wire mesh which is positioned over a collecting tray. Remove the tray when the wax melts into it but before the wax is hot enough to vaporize. Much of the wax and accompanying problems with fumes can be eliminated in this manner.

Using tongs, place the investment flask into the furnace over a wire mesh or on a ceramic stilt, with the sprue opening facing downwards (figure 4–23). The mesh or stilt allows air to enter the flask and the gases and wax to escape.

As a precaution, the flask is placed in a cold or slightly preheated furnace and gradually brought up in stages to maximum burnout temperature (1250°F–1350°F, or 677°C–732°C). The accompanying table indicates conservative times for burnout of the different size flasks. Note that the larger the flask, the longer the burnout period. To preserve the investment, the temperature within the furnace should never exceed 1350°F (732°C).

Suggested Wax Elimination Burnout Cycles

For flasks up to 2½ × 2½" (6.3 × 6.3 cm) 5 hour cycle	For flasks up to 3½ × 4" (8.5 × 10 cm) 8 hour cycle	For flasks up to 4 × 8" (10 × 20 cm) 12 hour cycle
Preheat furnace to to 300° F (150° C)	Preheat furnace to 300° F (150° C)	Preheat furnace to 300° F (150° C)
1 hour at 300° F (150° C)	2 hours at 300° F (150° C)	2 hours at 300 ° F (150° C)
1 hour at 700° F (370° C)	2 hours at 700° F (370° C)	2 hours at 600° F (315° C)
2 hours at 1350° F (732° C)	3 hours at 1350° F (732° C)	2 hours at 900° F (482° C)
1 hour - reduce to proper flask casting temperature	1 hour - reduce to proper flask casting temperature	4 hours at 1350° F (732° C)
		2 hours - reduce to proper flask casting temperature

Courtesy of Kerr Manufacturing Company.

Before you reduce the temperature, remove the flask with tongs and be sure the wax has entirely burned away. Complete elimination of the wax may be detected when the investment turns white and clean. The presence of dark patches on the investment indicates insufficient burnout (figure 4–24).

When burnout is complete, the investment is brought down to the proper temperature for casting by lowering the temperature in the furnace. It takes at least one-half hour for the temperature of the investment to drop to the lower temperature of the furnace. The accompanying casting temperature table indicates the temperatures of molten metal and the suggested flask temperatures for casting.

Casting Temperatures

Alloy	Metal Temperature		Flask Temperature	
	°F	°C	°F	°C
Silver	1750–1775	954–968	800	427
Gold 10 KY	1850	1010	950	510
Gold 14 KY	1825	996	900	482
Gold 10 KW	2025	1107	1000	538
Gold 14 KW	1925	1052	950	510
Bronze	1950	1066	900	482

Note: Casting temperature will vary slightly depending upon the particular alloy used. Flask temperature will vary depending upon size of casting.
Pure silver melts at 1762° F (961° C). Pure gold melts at 1945° F (1063° C).

Courtesy of Kerr Manufacturing Company.

FIG. 4–23   Place the flask in the furnace for burnout. *Courtesy of Kerr Manufacturing Co.*

FIG. 4–24   Flask with (left) insufficient burnout and (right) sufficient burnout. *Courtesy of Kerr Manufacturing Co.*

Casting is done immediately after the flask is removed from the furnace. The flask must not be allowed to cool and may not be reheated.

For situations where casting must be done quickly, it is possible, though risky, to burnout in less time than those indicated in the chart. Cristobalite investment is used to reduce the possibility of cracking. The small flask is placed in the furnace and gradually brought up to 600°F (315°C) over a period of 1 hour. In the second hour, the temperature is raised to 1250°F (677°C) and held at this temperature for an additional hour.

Centrifugal Casting

Materials. Centrifugal casting machine, casting tongs, torch with a large tip, borax, poker, metal for casting, pail of water, stiff brush.

The centrifugal casting machine forces molten metal into the mold by centrifugal force. The casting machine is bolted to a level, sturdy surface and surrounded by a metal shield to protect the jeweler from flying molten metal.

The main portion of the casting machine is the casting arm. The crucible and casting cradle are on one end of the casting arm and the counterweights are on the other end. Before burnout, balance the casting arm by placing the invested flask in the casting cradle with the sprue opening facing the center of the machine. Push the crucible containing the measured amount of metal tightly against the flask. Adjust the counterweights on the opposite end of the arm until the two ends of the arm are balanced. Tighten the central screw when the arm can be easily tipped in either direction by gently touching one end. After balancing, wind the arm approximately three times (see manufacturer's instructions) and hold it under tension by raising the pin. (Balancing is done before burnout so that the hot flask may be cast immediately after it is removed from the furnace.)

To cast, melt the metal in the crucible with a torch. Add a touch of borax as the metal melts. Remove the hot flask from the furnace with tongs and place it in the casting cradle. With the flask held tightly between the crucible and the metal back plate, continue heating the metal (figure 4–25). Test the metal with a poker to be certain that it is molten all the way to the bottom of the crucible. The molten metal will shine.

Before releasing the arm, be certain that the section of the casting arm that holds the flask is at right angles to the counterweight section. This "break" in the arm will reduce the risk of spilling molten metal as the arm begins to spin. With the torch still heating the metal, push the casting arm back, allowing the pin to drop. Do not release the arm until you are ready simultaneously to remove the torch. The arm will spin, forcing the metal into the mold. Allow the arm to continue spinning until it stops by itself.

After the metal has cooled for a few minutes, remove the flask with tongs from the casting machine and immerse it in a pail of water (figure 4–26). Due to the drastic change in temperature, the investment will explode away from the metal, leaving the cast piece loose in the pail. Clean the casting with a stiff brush. Saw off the sprues with a jeweler's saw (figure 4–27) and then pickle, file, emery and polish the piece.

FIG. 4–25   Mount the flask in the cradle and heat the metal in the crucible. Centrifugal force will force the metal into the mold. *Courtesy of Kerr Manufacturing Co.*

FIG. 4–26   To free the cast piece from the investment, place the flask into a pail of water. *Courtesy of Kerr Manufacturing Co.*

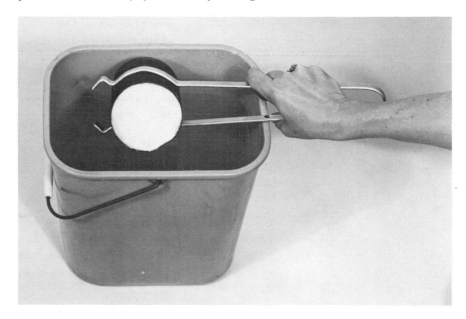

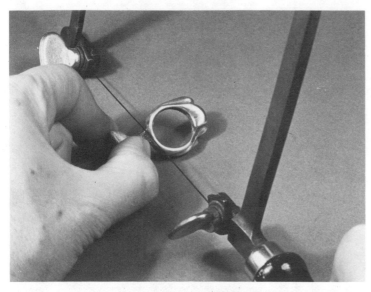

FIG. 4–27 Remove sprues with a jeweler's saw.

FIG. 4–28 Completed cast piece.

Steam Casting

Steam pressure is another means of forcing molten metal into a mold. The mold for steam casting is made in the same manner as in centrifugal casting with one important difference: the sprued model is mounted on a wire, which is inserted into a sprue base that has been modified to create a crucible right in the mold.

Mounting the Model

For steam casting only, the main sprue should terminate in a small wax ball. Use a modeling tool to add and shape the wax. Then insert one end of a 14-gauge metal wire into the wax ball and the other end into the modified sprue base. Secure the wire to the base with a piece of soft wax. See figure 4–29.

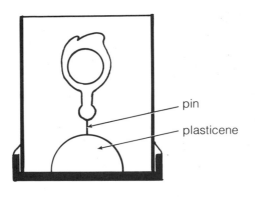

FIG. 4–29   Invested flask
for steam casting.

To modify the sprue base, add plasticene around the conical sprue base to form a hemisphere. This will create a hemispherical cavity in the mold when the base and pin are removed before burnout. After burnout, the metal will be heated directly in this cavity. The narrow channel created by the pin will prevent metal from running into the mold as it is being melted in the crucible. When pressure is applied, however, the molten metal will be forced through the channel.

Constructing the Steam Casting Device

Materials.   Jar lid, somewhat larger than the mold; ½″ (1.3 cm) diameter dowel, approximately 6″ (15 cm) long; newspaper, nail or screw; scissors; bucket of water.

A steam casting device is shown in figure 4–30. To construct it, use a screw or nail to attach a 6″ (15 cm) piece of dowel to the top side of a large jar lid. The jar lid must be larger than the mold so that you can be sure of getting it flush against the mold in the quick action of casting. There is no time to position the lid. The first action must therefore be accurate. The screw or nail connection

FIG. 4–30   The steam caster.

should be loose enough to insure flexibility and a tight, flush fit over the mold.

Line the inside of the lid with several layers of newspaper. When this is assembled, dip the caster into a bucket of water to soak the newspaper. In casting, the steam pressure will come from this wet newspaper.

Preparing and Casting the Metal

Materials. Charcoal crucible, flux (borax), poker, metal for casting, flask tongs, torch with large tip, steam caster, bucket of water.

In steam casting, you will be heating the metal directly in the crucible that has been created in the flask, rather than melting the metal in a separate crucible. It is therefore best to prepare the metal for casting by melting the metal scraps into a slug. To do this, carve a depression in a charcoal block. Place the scrap metal into the depression and heat with a hot flame until the metal flows together into a slug.

Transfer the cooled slug to the crucible cavity of the hot flask just after you remove the flask from the furnace. Using the same torch tip, reheat the metal until it melts within the crucible. Remove any sludge that forms on the molten metal surface with a poker. Flux the metal by dipping the hot poker into borax and transferring it to the molten metal. When the metal is shiny and completely melted, remove the torch and simultaneously apply the steam caster to the top of the flask. For a good casting, the caster should be held directly above the flask and applied just at the moment when the torch is removed. Any hesitation will result in an incomplete casting.

To remove the casting from the investment, after the metal has cooled a few minutes, place the hot flask into a bucket of water. The investment will explode in the water from the extreme change in temperature, leaving the cast metal piece loose in the bucket.

Clean the casting with a stiff brush, and saw the sprues off with a jeweler's saw. Then the piece is pickled, filed, emeried, and polished.

Casting Found Objects

Any object that will burn out totally in the furnace can be cast using the same method as for lost wax casting. Among the objects that can be cast are bugs, pinecones, small plastic toys, plastic utensils, and food. A plastic lidded box can be cast in two pieces to obtain a metal box with a lid which will fit perfectly on its base. In order to stiffen objects such as bugs, coat the object with varnish or hair

FIG. 4–31   Ellen Reiben. "Progression." Sterling silver. The horses are cast from toy figures. *Courtesy of the artist. Photo by Joan Marcus.*

FIG. 4–32   Richard Mawdsley. "Wonder Woman in her Bicentenial Finery." Pendant of sterling silver, pearls, and smoky quartz. Fabricated with cast head. *Courtesy of the artist.*

spray. In this way, the weak areas such as the legs will have less chance of breaking in the casting process.

Sprue found objects in the same manner as a wax model. Where most found-object castings go wrong is in insufficient burnout. Often a longer burnout period is necessary. Any remaining ashes should be gently tapped out of the mold after burnout.

THE ARTIST SPEAKS: ELLEN REIBEN

Often I incorporate cast toys and construction techniques in my work. I tend to think and work in series. What is important to me is the use of a found object in such a way that the toy image is not an end in itself but merely a springboard for an idea. Therefore, the image is used as an element in the work just as a stone or other object might be used. I'm not particularly interested in carving an image myself, although if I can't find what I want I occasionally do. My concern lies in a playful use of a treasured object or found toy.

Cast "Granulation"

True granulation is a difficult process to master. However, the look of granulation can be closely imitated by the following process. In granulation, the surface of the wax is covered with tiny balls which create a textured surface on the metal. To achieve this effect in casting, styrene balls purchased from a plastics manufacturer or taken from a child's stuffed toy can be adhered to the wax surface using tincture of green soap. The soap is brushed onto the balls and wax and allowed to dry, creating a bond between them. A beautiful surface can be achieved using one or several size balls.

Custom Casting

Many jewelers do not wish to be bothered with casting their jewelry or do not wish to invest in the necessary equipment. They send their work out to be cast. Consult your Yellow Pages or crafts magazines for a listing of casters in your area. If delivery is to be made through the mail, take great care to protect the wax model from breakage. Wrap the model in plastic wrap so that it will not shake around within the box. Hand delivery is a lot less risky.

No special preparation of the model is necessary for custom casting. The caster will return the metal piece with sprues attached and the surface unpolished. Sprues must be sawed off, filed, and polished to complete the piece. The caster can also make a rubber mold of the piece should you wish to cast more than one.

Surface Texture

5

DESIGNING YOUR WORK: TEXTURE

Texture is the character of a surface, and it presents a rich arena for creative exploration. Although a highly polished surface is suitable for many pieces, one need not automatically shine everything. In many cases, a matted, stamped, engraved, or otherwise textured surface may be more faithful to the overall concept of the work.

By concentrating on our sense of touch, we may become more sensitive to the variety of textures in our ordinary experience. Trees, animals, stones, food, plants, and machines may all be experienced as texture.

We encounter texture in two ways. Visual texture refers to the two-dimensional surface patterns that we see: small variations in shape, line, color, and value. A photograph of a piece of bark will feel smooth if touched, but it will appear to be rough. A technique such as Mokume, a Japanese technique of lamintaing metals, is an example of visual texture. (See page 120 for a description of Mokume.)

Actual texture, on the other hand, refers to what we feel when a surface is touched. In jewelry, we are dealing for the most part with actual texture.

The effect of light on actual texture is significant. The angle at which light strikes the surface will create variety in the value and length of the shadows. Texture may be used for contrast between rough and smooth as well as dark and light areas. Specific portions of a piece may be textured for emphasis or variety, or to imitate another surface.

Reticulation

Reticulation is a method of texturing metal using the heat of a torch to alter the surface of the metal. Reticulation occurs when a layer of fine metal, such as pure silver or gold, is built up on the surface of a metal alloy. The metal alloy beneath the surface has a lower melting point and will thus melt before the outer surface. This difference in the rates of melting causes the inner core to melt and the outer surface to ripple.

A reticulated surface is made on a sheet of 820 silver or 14K gold. (See *Sources of Supplies* for where to purchase reticulation silver.) A greater amount of copper is contained in 820 silver (820 parts silver, 180 parts copper) than in sterling (925 parts silver, 75 parts copper). Sterling silver or other silver alloys may also be used, but results may not be as successful. Because this process is not totally controllable and does cause shrinkage, it is best to work with a large sheet of metal and select sections to be cut out and incorporated in your piece of jewelry.

FIG. 5–1   Barbara Mail. "Homage to the Fan Lady-Child." Fibula of fine and sterling silver, reticulation silver, 14K gold, broken optical lens, tintype, and lace. *Courtesy of the artist.*

FIG. 5–2   Linda Threadgill. "Landform Box." Sterling and 825 silver (top). Reticulated and fabricated. *Courtesy of the artist.*

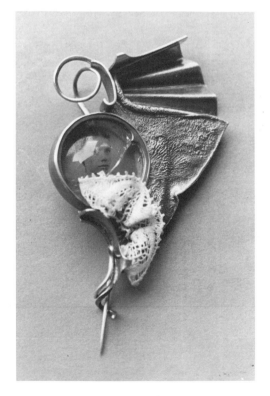

Preparing the Metal

Before reticulating, a layer of pure metal is raised on the surface by annealing and pickling the metal a minimum of five times. The thicker this coat of pure metal, the better the results will be. Brass brush with soapy water after each pickling, except on the final pickling. Keep all dirt, including fingerprints, off the metal.

Reticulating the Metal

For best results, use a gas-air torch for reticulation. Heat the metal with a hot torch until it begins to ripple. The force of the gas-air torch flame can be used to advantage here to make patterns in the metal. The size, distance from the metal, and angle of the torch, as well as the content of the metal, will contribute to the results. You have only one shot at reticulation, and work must be done quickly before the outer pure metal surface also melts. If a hole develops in the metal, it may be used as part of your design (a stone might be set into it, for example), or other sections of the sheet can be used.

Finishing

After the desired sections have been cut out and pickled, they can be polished with a brass brush dipped in soapy water. Liver of sulfur can be used to color the recessed surface, and the raised texture can be polished for contrast.

It is advisable to use cold connections (those requiring no soldering or heating) to attach reticulated metal to the main part of your jewelry. Because of the convoluted surface and the great stress placed on the metal in this process, the reticulated metal is more difficult to work than the original metal. A limited amount of forming and soldering can be done, however.

Fusing

Fusing is a method of joining metals with heat, but without using solder. The surfaces of the metals to be joined actually melt and penetrate each other. Care must be taken to use the proper amount of heat so that the fusion is controlled. Excess heat will cause the metal to melt completely, forming a puddle of molten metal. A lack of heat will prevent the metals from adhering. Fusion can be done with a torch or kiln as the heat source. The kiln allows for even heating, and kilns with pyrometers permit greater control of the process. The torch allows you to concentrate heat on specific areas.

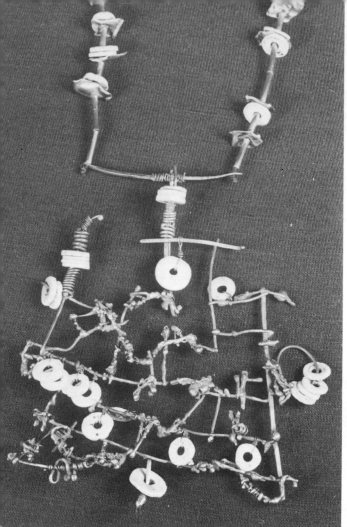

FIG. 5–3　Dorothy Lavine. Sterling silver and ostrich eggshell. Fused. *Courtesy of the artist.*

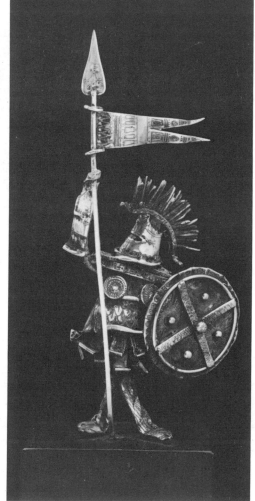

FIG. 5–4　Mary Ann Scherr. Sterling silver chessman. 4″ × 10″ (10.2 × 25.4 cm). Fused silver, engraved, and hollow-constructed. *Courtesy of the artist.*

Fusion can be done with metal scraps, sheet, wire, or any form of metal. Texture can be built up on a sheet of metal by adding small metal scraps and wire after first heating the sheet almost to the melting point. In this way a coil or wire can be used to "draw" on the metal; the torch will fuse the wire as it is fed onto the sheet.

Combining fused and stamped or chased textures on a single piece makes a lovely combination of flowing and sharply defined forms.

For fusion to take place, both metals must be brought to the proper temperature *at the same time*. Therefore, larger pieces or metals with a higher melting point must receive more heat than smaller pieces of metal with a lower melting point. A keen eye will be your best guide. Pickling and fluxing the metal will greatly aid in the fusing process.

Try heating a variety of different sizes, forms, and types of metals. See what happens when you heat the end of a wire or the edge of a piece of sheet metal. Perhaps the results from overheating specific areas of a sheet will be suitable for your design. Try pressing a metal pick or other metal object into the molten metal to see what happens.

Making a Fused Ring

Materials. 14-gauge round wire, ring mandrel, ring sizer, pliers, flux, pickle, charcoal block or carbon ring stick, soldering pick, torch, liver of sulfur, polishing equipment.

Approximately one foot (30 cm) of 14-gauge silver wire is used to make the ring in this project. Begin by pickling the wire. Bend the wire around the correct size on the ring mandrel to form the ring shank. (Use a ring sizer to determine the correct size; its numbers correspond to the sizes on the mandrel.) Bend the remaining wire with pliers to form the face of the ring (figure 5–5). Flux and fuse the ring on a charcoal block or ring stick (figure 5–6). Wire may be added and heated with the torch until it is fused in a pleasing design. After fusing, pickle the piece.

A colorant such as liver of sulfur may be applied after polishing. Raised areas can then be polished again, creating greater contrast between raised and recessed surfaces.

Freezing Molten Metal

A quick and simple method of forming metal with a textured surface is to pour molten metal over ice water. The liquid metal freezes into exciting forms upon contact with the cold water (figure 5–8).

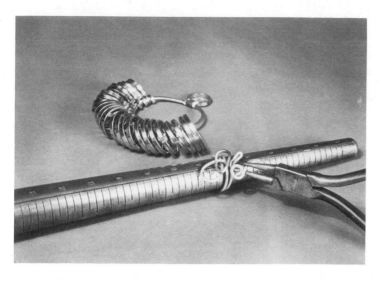

FIG. 5–5 Twist the wire around a ring mandrel and bend the remaining wire into a design using pliers.

FIG. 5–6 Flux and heat the metal until it fuses. A charcoal ring stick supports the ring nicely during fusion.

FIG. 5–7 Completed fused ring.

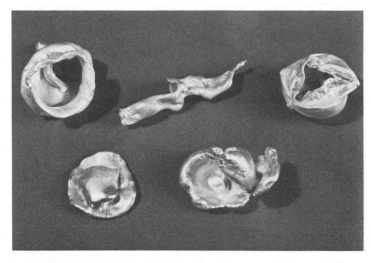

FIG. 5–8 Forms created by pouring molten metal into cold water.

FIG. 5–9 To freeze molten metal into unusual forms, melt in a charcoal crucible with a touch of borax, and pour into ice water.

Materials. Metal scraps, ice water in a large container, charcoal block, tongs, borax, torch, pickle, polishing equipment.

It is important to pickle the metal before heating it to a molten state. Melt the metal in a depression that has been carved in a charcoal block. Add a touch of borax as a fluxing agent. Using tongs to hold the charcoal crucible, pour the molten metal into a deep jar filled with ice and water (figure 5–9). As the molten metal splashes over the ice, it solidifies instantly into a free form shape. No two shapes are identical, and a great variety of forms can be created in this way. Experiment by pouring the metal from different heights into different size and temperature water containers. Unsuccessful pieces can be remelted.

The results of this process can be used as an addition to a constructed piece, fused together to form a larger work, or simply as they are. Consider the addition of a pearl or stone. Baroque pearls are similar in form and can be an interesting addition to a piece made by this method.

Rolling Mill Prints

A simple way to transfer texture onto metal is by using the pressure of a rolling mill (figure 5–10). Materials such as screening, sections of etching plates, lace, coins, cloth, and leaves can be rolled between two pieces of metal to leave an impression (figure 5–11). The second piece of metal is necessary to protect the rollers from materials that could damage them. Linear designs can be made by using wire or string, or other linear materials.

Begin by annealing and pickling the metal. Be certain that all surfaces are clean and dry to protect the rollers. Remove the pickling solution by rinsing the metal in baking soda and water. Any pickle that remains on the metal may corrode the rollers. It is also advisable to protect the rollers further with a coating of petroleum jelly.

Adjust the rollers so they grip the metal rather tightly and there is some resistance when turning the handle. Roll the materials through the mill. The metal size will change because this process stretches the metal in the direction of the movement through the mill.

The resulting textured metal sheet may be used in any number of ways. A simple but effective ring band may be made by cutting a strip of this texture and soldering the seam.

To add color contrast to your textured print, flux and flood the impression with solder of a contrasting metal. The sheet metal is

FIG. 5–10   Rolling mill.
Courtesy of Allcraft.

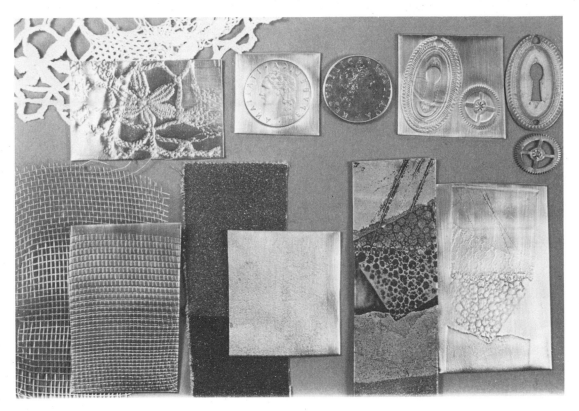

FIG. 5–11 Textures created by running lace, a coin, a brass keyhole and watch part, screening, emery paper, and an etched plate through the rolling mill.

then filed down to remove excess solder, leaving the pattern of the two metals. It is sometimes helpful to bend the sheet temporarily into a gentle curve, making it easier to get to all areas for filing.

Stamping and Chasing

Use a chasing hammer to strike a variety of chasing and stamping tools, small dapping punches, and nails filed to different shapes to create a variety of surface textures (figure 5–13). The metal can be supported on wood, lead, linoleum, pitch, or leather. These supports will allow the metal to stretch when struck, producing a deep impression.

The tools may be held at different angles or rotated while being struck to increase the versatility of each tool. One impression may be made over another. Tools usually used for other purposes, such as a center punch or alphabet and number stamps, may be used to create textures which read no longer as figures but rather as patterns. Metal design and signature stamps may be custom made (see *Sources of Supplies*).

FIG. 5–12   Carey Smith. Brooch fabricated from sterling silver, brass, bronze, Derlin, and Lexan. 1973. *Courtesy of the artist.*

FIG. 5–13   Textures created with various tools: chasing tools, stamp, center punch, matting tool, dapping punch, letter stamps.

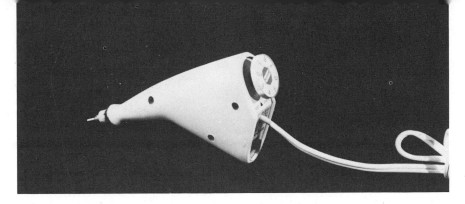

FIG. 5–14   Electric engraving tool. *Courtesy of Allcraft*.

Using an Electric Engraving Tool

With practice, controlled, shallow surface textures can be produced with an electric engraving tool (figure 5–14). The vibration creates tiny dots so close together that they read as lines and texture. Try varying the speed of the vibration and the speed at which the tool is moved across the metal to achieve different effects. And try going over engraved lines with other engraved lines. The piece in figure 5–15 is an example of a surface that was engraved with an electric tool.

Etching

Materials.   Metal to be etched (silver, copper, or brass), asphaltum varnish (or paraffin, beeswax, nail polish, masking tape, or contact paper), nitric acid or other mordant, etching needles, small paint brush, copper tongs, baking soda or household ammonia, turpentine to thin varnish, a feather.

Etching is a method of creating surface designs or texture in metal by the use of a mordant (usually an acid), which is used to "bite" or corrode the metal, thus removing it in selected areas. A *resist* is first applied to the metal to prevent corrosion in places where the action of the acid is not desired. All nonprotected areas will be corroded to the extent to which they are allowed to remain in the acid.

The Resist

The resist, usually asphaltum, is applied by dripping, dipping the metal into it, or, most usually, by brushing it on. The entire piece of metal may be coated with asphaltum and the design scratched through this layer of varnish, thus exposing the metal. This process

FIG. 5–15 Mary Ann Scherr. "Applique necklace." 14K gold, sterling silver, and black opal. Surface fully engraved with an electric tool. *Courtesy of the artist.*

is called *intaglio*. Very delicate work can be done in this way. When the asphaltum is brushed onto areas to create a raised design, and the background is left unprotected to be eaten by the acid, the technique is called *relief etching*. Both techniques may be used on a single piece.

To begin, apply the asphaltum to the pickled metal on areas that you want to remain unetched. (This includes the back and sides of the piece.) Allow the asphaltum to dry.

Safety Precautions

When making the acid bath, *always add the acid to the water*. This will minimize the reaction between the two substances and will prevent burning. When working with acid, wear rubber gloves to protect your hands from burns, and use a special respirator with a filter specifically made for acid mists. Goggles should also be worn. Keep a neutralizer such as baking soda or household ammonia mixed with water handy in case acid spills or splatters on your clothes or body. Good ventilation is essential.

The Mordant

To make the mordant, mix nitric acid and water in a glass tray. For sterling silver, use 1 part acid to 3 parts water. For copper or brass, use 1 part acid to 2 parts water. These proportions give a relatively strong mordant. Actual proportions may vary with individual preference. Use a separate acid bath for each different metal. Be sure to place the metal face up so that you will be able to see how the acid is acting on it.

The metal will not be etched if too little acid is used, which will be evident if few or no bubbles can be seen rising from the exposed metal. A high ratio of acid to water will create a faster etch, but the line will not be as clean and there will be considerable undercutting. Acid that is too strong will also tend to lift the resist. If this happens, the piece must be removed from the acid, washed in running water, and dried. Then use paraffin or beeswax to patch the resist; because they will dry quickly, they are used in this case rather than asphaltum. If too much acid is used, it will be evident by the emission of a brown gas. It is dangerous to breathe this gas.

The Etching Process

When the acid begins to corrode the metal, small bubbles will form on the areas being etched. These bubbles will impede the etching and should be brushed away with a feather or by agitating the acid.

Do not feather if you want a rough texture. Check the piece for the depth of the bite and to be certain that no resist has been lifted. If bubbles form on the area that you want to be resisted, remove the piece, wash and dry it, and apply new resist on those areas as described above. Temperature, length of time that the metal is exposed to the acid, and especially the strength of the acid will determine how long the metal must remain in the bath.

When the work is etched, remove it from the bath, wash it in running water, and remove the asphaltum varnish with turpentine and a soft cloth.

Combining Metals

6

Color can be added to jewelry in many ways: through enameling, painting, the application of heat and chemicals, and with the use of gems, plastics, and other materials. And the color of the metal itself can be exploited, with different metals providing the jeweler with a wide selection of colors.

Marriage of Metals

One method of combining metals is to solder one piece of metal next to another. For example, strips of sheet metal or rectangular and square wire can be soldered together to form a single, striped sheet. Juxtapose different metals of varying widths to add variety.

Materials. 18- × 30-gauge copper and silver cloisonné wire, 18-gauge square wire, 18-gauge rectangular wire of varying widths and metals, two pairs of pliers, T pins, hard sheet solder, soldering and hand polishing equipment, flat charcoal block; soldering pick and files.

First, the metals should be annealed, cleaned, and flattened. To avoid overheating, the cloisonné wire is coiled before annealing. After annealing it is straightened by pulling the wire taut with two pairs of pliers or pliers and a vise (figure 6–3). Handle the wire as little as possible in order to keep it clean and flat. Any kinks will make soldering difficult. Pickle all metal including the solder before soldering.

Cut the wire into strips approximately 1″ (2.5 cm) long, which is a convenient size to work with. Line up the strips in the desired order on a charcoal block that has been filed or sanded flat.

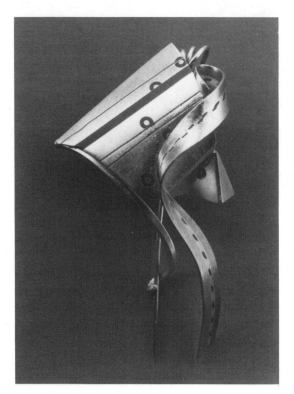

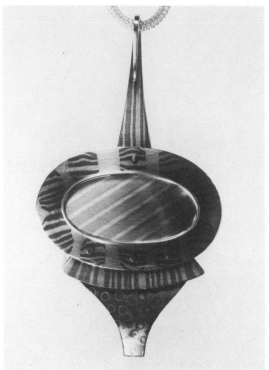

FIG. 6–1 Barbara Mail. Fibula of mixed metals. *Courtesy of the artist.*

FIG. 6–2 Chuck Evans. Pendant of sterling silver, copper, and 14K gold. Multimetal lamination, inlay of the laminant, and forged laminated rod. *Courtesy of the artist.*

Charcoal is a good surface for this type of work because it retains heat well. Arrange the strips so that the resulting sheet of combined metals will be an even, 18-gauge-thick layer. Stick two T pins into the charcoal to provide a barrier against which the metals may be pushed together. Before soldering, coat all metal, including the solder, with flux.

To solder, heat the metals to soldering temperature. (Handy Flux clears at this temperature.) Apply strips of solder perpendicular to the strips of metal. Place the solder close to the ends of the metals rather than toward the middle (figure 6–4). Use enough solder to flood the metal completely and thoroughly fill the seams between the wires. Keep the strips of metal in close contact by pushing them gently against the T pins with a soldering pick. If you push too hard, the metal strips will fold together. After the solder has flowed, hold the metal strips flat and close together until the solder has hardened. Then, flip the metal over and heat until the solder is drawn through and has penetrated the entire piece.

To finish, pickle the soldered metal, file, and polish with

FIG. 6–3 Straighten the wire by stretching it between a vise and pliers or between two pairs of pliers.

progressively finer grits of emery paper, working down from 240 to 600 grit. The metal may be held on a dop stick for easy handling of small work (see below).

The sheet of mixed metals may be used as is or cut and resoldered to form a new pattern. A checkerboard pattern, for example, can be made with strips of married metal that have been sliced perpendicular to the original strips. These strips are soldered together so that adjacent squares are of different colors.

The piece by Gayle Saunders in figure 6–5 is an example of mixed metals.

Chemical Coloring

Liver of sulfur can be used to increase contrast between the metals. The different metals will react differently to the chemical treatment, and the color contrast between them will increase. For example, if you are working with copper and sterling silver, dip the piece quickly into the liver of sulfur and rinse immediately. The copper will darken faster than the silver. Experiment to find the best chemical strength and the amount of exposure time needed for each combination of metals.

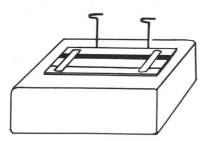

FIG. 6–4 Line up the metal strips on the charcoal block and press them tightly against the T pins. Place strips of solder near both ends.

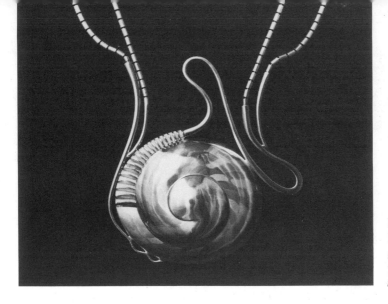

FIG. 6–5   Gayle Saunders.
Pendant of sterling silver, 14K
green and rose gold, and 18K
yellow gold. 1977. *Courtesy of
the artist.*

Using a Dop Stick

A dop stick may be used to hold pieces that are too small to be held easily while sanding. To make a dop stick, use a wooden dowel or an unsharpened pencil. Melt flake shellac on a piece of foil or similar surface, using a low flame or match. Very little heat is needed to melt the shellac. Press and roll one end of the stick in the melted shellac. While the shellac is still warm, press it onto the metal so that the stick is perpendicular to the metal (figure 6–6). The shellac will harden as it cools and will hold the work firmly.

Making a Tube of Mixed Metals

To make a tube of mixed metals, you will need two pieces of 20- or 18-gauge-square annealed wire of contrasting colors. The two ends of the wires may be soldered together. Wrap the wires tightly around a mandrel, a small dowel, or a jump-ring winder. Remove the wire from the mandrel and flux it. Working on a charcoal block with a groove filed to hold the wire, solder with wire solder from the coil until the metal forms a solid tube (see figure 6–7). Use enough solder to flood the metal completely. Then file and polish the tube as described above.

THE ARTIST SPEAKS: GAYLE SAUNDERS

I twist long lengths of wire of different colored metals. I cut this twisted length into shorter pieces and solder them side by side. Then I roll all of these soldered wires flat through the rolling mill, thus making a sheet of patterned metal. From this sheet I then form and fabricate a piece. Sometimes I further laminate this sheet with other metals, depending on the desired pattern. Because of all the vari-

FIG. 6–6 Use melted flake shellac to hold a small piece on a dop stick for easy handling during sanding.

ables, the countless ways in which you can twist wires, the different thicknesses of wire, the varied directions in which you can roll it through the mill, and how many times it is rolled, the variety of patterns is endless.

THE ARTIST SPEAKS: ENID KAPLAN

My recent series of one-of-a-kind jewelry explores the textured contrasts and color interplay of geometrically patterned married metals with woods, semiprecious stones, and acrylics. In almost all of my work, I try to establish a tension between contrasting elements. Sometimes the tension will be between the controlled geometry of the married metal surfaces and the fluidity of the forms that contain them. In other cases, the tension will be created when the precise surface is disrupted by the introduction of an organic element, such as a drawn line or irregular channel. This recalls to me the same sort of peaceful irony I find in the walls of the ancient ruins, which have been mocked by time and whose forces have disrupted their static perfection.

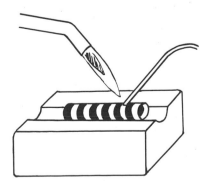

FIG. 6–7 Place the coiled wire in a grooved charcoal block and flood the tube completely with solder.

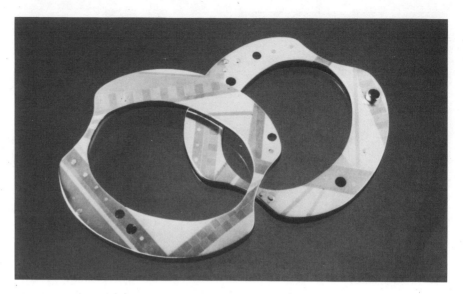

FIG. 6–8   Enid Kaplan. Bangle bracelets of Plexiglas, 14K gold, brass, nickel, copper, and citrine. *Courtesy of the artist.*

Making a Construction with Married Metals

Figure 6–8 illustrates Enid Kaplan's work, and the following is her method for making a construction of married metals:

1. The design is carefully drawn on graph paper with colored pencils, each color representing a different metal. Shapes are designed so that pieces fit together like a jigsaw puzzle.

2. The pieces of the design are cut from different colored metals of 14- or 16-gauge sheet metal with a jeweler's saw. Each piece should be carefully filed so that the edges fit perfectly. A good fit is crucial when marrying metals to avoid spaces and pits.

3. Small groupings of pieces are made so that no more than five or six pieces are married at one time. The pieces will move slightly during soldering, and it is difficult to rearrange them when too many pieces are being worked at the same time.

4. Each grouping is arranged on a flat, clean charcoal block. Pieces are fluxed and heated gradually. If they move, they can be repositioned with a soldering pick. When pieces are hot enough to melt the solder, use medium-wire solder and touch the solder to the joints. Be generous with the solder; the excess will be sanded off. Pickle until clean.

5. All of the groupings are then soldered together to form a larger shape. Again, medium solder is used.

6. This large shape is then soldered to a backing of 22- or 24-gauge sheet using medium solder. Support the piece on wire mesh placed on a tripod and heat from below. Pickle.

7. The desired shape is sawed out using a jeweler's saw and filed at the edges. The piece is hammered flat with a rawhide mallet.

8. The married metal surface is sanded with a disc sander.

9. Pits or holes are filled with easy solder.

10. The piece is sanded again with a disc sander and then with various grits of emery paper: 120, 220, 320, 400, 500, and 600.

11. The edges are polished and the surface is finished with paste wax and a polishing cloth.

12. The completed married metal surface is either bezel-set like a stone or riveted to another surface, as in the bangle bracelet by Enid Kaplan shown in the color section.

Embedding Metal in Solder

Metals of contrasting colors can be combined in an infinite variety of patterns by embedding them in solder, backed by a sheet of solid metal. The pattern is created by twisting contrasting wires, juxtaposing different colored wires, embedding brass or copper screening, laying down scraps in a mosaic pattern, spiraling twisted or single wires, knitting or crocheting wire, or whatever you may think up.

To embed the metal, begin by cleaning and fluxing all metal, including the solder. Place the sheet metal on a tripod with a layer of sheet solder, slightly smaller, on top of it. The metal wires or scraps to be embedded are then placed on top of the solder in the desired pattern. Try not to leave gaps between the metal pieces. Large gaps cannot be filled with solder and will keep the surface from being smooth. Then heat the metal mainly from below to protect the smaller pieces of metal from overheating and melting. If necessary, use a soldering pick to coax the solder into gaps. Extra solder can be fed into the work if necessary. When all gaps are filled and the top surface is level, pickle the piece.

After soldering, you will have to do a lot of filing and sanding to remove excess solder and expose the pattern beneath it. Sand with progressively finer grit emery paper until the surface is smoothed down from 240 to 600 grit.

The finished piece may be gently formed, cut into sections, and resoldered to form a more complex form, or it may be incorporated in a piece "as is."

Wire Inlay: Making a Tie Tack

This is one method of making fine line inlays in sheet metal.

Materials. 3/0 or 4/0 saw blades, jeweler's saw, drill with bits of the same size as wire to be inlayed as dots, bezel wire or copper

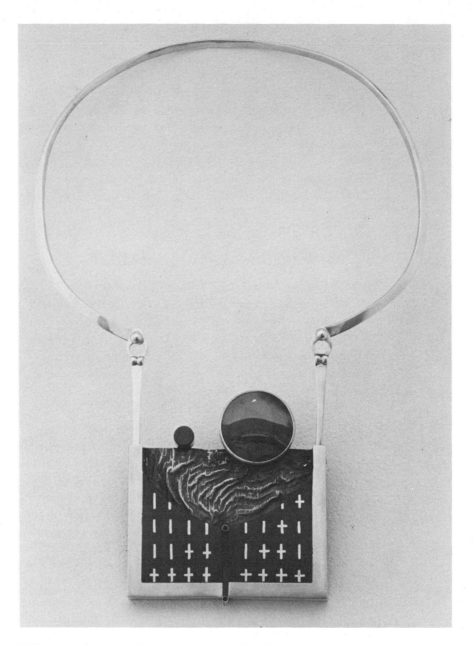

FIG. 6–9 Gene and Hiroko Pijanowski. Pendant of sterling silver, brass, Shakudo (Japanese alloy), silk, thread, and jasper. Constructed, inlayed, and reticulated. *Courtesy of the artists.*

or fine silver cloisonné wire for lines, bezel shears, sheet of 18-gauge metal of a contrasting color for background, round wire of contrasting color for dots, mallet, two pairs of pliers, solder, flat charcoal block, flux; soldering pick, torch with a #3 tip, ring clamp, dop stick, tie-tack findings, pickling and polishing equipment.

FIG. 6–10 To inlay a piece of wire to form a dot, drill a hole the same size as the wire.

Making an Inlayed Dot

To create an inlayed dot, use round wire of the desired diameter. The wire is inlayed perpendicular to the sheet through a hole drilled to the same diameter as the wire (figure 6–10). It is important to drill the hole equal to or smaller than the size of the wire. A small hole may be filed larger using a round needle file. Cut the wire so that it protrudes slightly beyond the sheet on the top and bottom and solder it in place, using enough solder to flood the seam. Excess wire can be filed off after soldering. All metal should be pickled before and after soldering.

FIG. 6–11 For line inlay, saw the line using a saw blade of the same width as the cloisonné wire being inlayed.

Line Inlay

When first planning your design, try to limit the lines to a few gentle curves. Too many lines may weaken the metal and make it difficult to keep flat. On a large piece, cut and solder one line before proceeding to the next.

To begin, flatten the sheet metal with a mallet. Next cut out the line according to your design using a 3/0 or 4/0 saw blade (figure 6–11). Cut internal lines by first drilling a hole to receive the saw blade. The cut line should be the same width as the cloisonné wire.

Use cloisonné or bezel wire (a very malleable wire of fine silver) to match the gauge of the sheet of metal. The wire must be annealed and straightened before inserting it into the cut channel. To prevent melting, wind the wire into a tight coil before annealing. Use a small torch tip and a low flame.

To straighten the annealed wire, stretch it between two pairs of pliers or between pliers and a vise, as shown in figure 6–3. This will pull out the kinks and permit the wire to fit easily into the sheet metal. The wire should be handled gently to keep it straight. Anneal the wire again after straightening and then pickle.

Before inserting the wire into the cut line in the sheet, anneal and flatten the sheet. When inserting the wire, leave a small amount protruding at the edge (figure 6–12). This can be easily cut off after soldering. Now flux the entire piece and place it on a block of flat charcoal. An old charcoal block can be filed or sanded flat. The back of the piece should be facing up so that the front remains level. Using hard solder, cover the areas to be soldered to flood the lines and fill in small gaps (figure 6–13). If necessary, use a soldering pick to help the solder flow around the lines. Be certain that all areas are filled with solder to the height of the sheet.

Next, clean the piece and remove excess solder by filing. A ring clamp is helpful for holding a small piece when filing (figure 6–14). File until the piece is a single smooth sheet. The entire sheet may be used, or sections may be cut out and incorporated in a piece.

Emery and polish to a matt finish; a high polish will not show the color contrast to its best advantage. Use a dop stick to hold small pieces while emerying (figure 6–15). Solder the finding onto the back to complete the tie tack (figures 6–16 and 6–17).

Inlay Variations

Interesting designs may be created with both line and dot inlay. Use different size dots, and try inlaying tubing to create an open dot, or fill the tubing with wire of a contrasting color to form concentric circles. Drilled holes may be filed square to accept square wire.

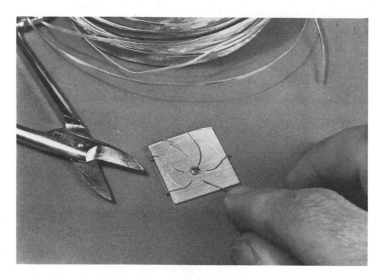

FIG. 6–12   Place the wires into the sawed and drilled spaces.

FIG. 6–13   Use plenty of solder to solder the wires in place and create a solid sheet of mixed metals.

FIG. 6–14   File to remove excess solder and make the surface level.

FIG. 6–15 Sand the surface smooth.

FIG. 6–16 Solder on the findings to make a tie tack.

FIG. 6–17 Completed tie tack.

Line and dot inlay may be done in wood and ivory as well as in metal. The hole is drilled partially through the material into which the wire is to be inlayed. Masking tape may be wound around the drill bit to act as a visual gauge in order to stop the drilling at the desired depth. Epoxy rather than solder is used to adhere the metal to the wood or ivory. After the epoxy has set, excess metal is filed down to the level of the material into which it has been inlayed.

Wire Inlaying by Pressure

Another method of creating lines of a contrasting color in metal is by inlaying the wire through pressure. A hammer or a rolling mill is used to force one metal into a larger background sheet of metal.

Wire, shot, screening, twisted wire, or small scraps of sheet metal may be inlayed by pressure. Clean and flux the selected metal and the background sheet. Now solder the inlay to the background sheet (figure 6–18).

After soldering, clean the work in pickle and scrape off the excess solder (figure 6–19). Now you are ready to press the wire and scraps into the sheet. To accomplish this, turn the sheet face down on a smooth metal surface plate. Hammer the metal sheet with a slightly domed planishing hammer until the front side of the metal is smooth (figure 6–20). If a rolling mill is available, run the piece through the mill until all of the metal is pressed into a single sheet of the same gauge as the original sheet.

After the metal is flattened, reheat it with the torch to make the solder flow into any unadhered areas. Add extra solder if necessary.

The piece is cleaned, filed, and sanded. A high polish is not recommended. A matt finish will emphasize the color contrast between the different metals.

For a piece such as this, a finding can be soldered onto the back to make a stickpin (figures 6 21 and 6–22).

Solder Inlay

Solder inlay is a process in which a depression is cut, filed, engraved, dapped, drilled, chased, or pressed into the metal and filled with solder of a contrasting color. The work is filed flush and finished as described in *Embedding Metal in Solder* earlier in this chapter.

THE ARTIST SPEAKS: GAYLE SAUNDERS

I am concerned with subtleties, with making connections. Time is moving so fast these days that we must be sensitive to changes in our patterns, we must look closer at our surroundings or we won't

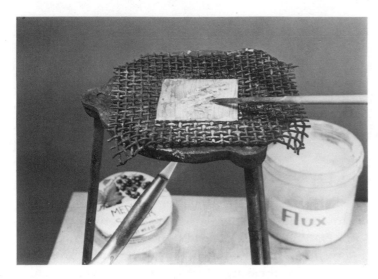

FIG. 6–18   Solder the wire onto the metal, heating mainly from below.

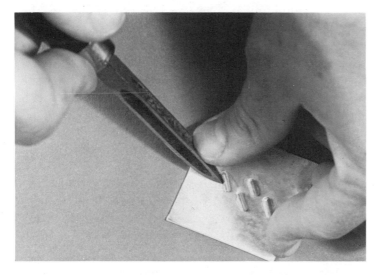

FIG. 6–19   Use a scraper to remove excess solder.

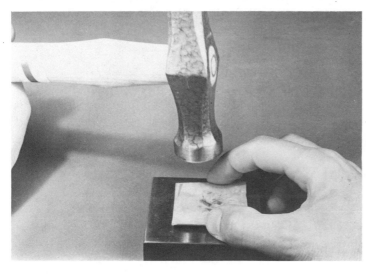

FIG. 6–20   Hammer the metal flat against a steel surface plate. Work with the soldered wire against the plate.

FIG. 6–21   Solder on the finding.

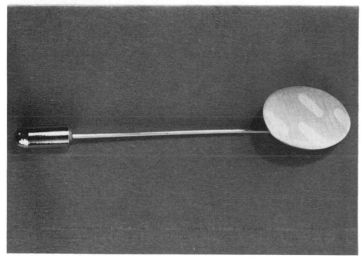

FIG. 6–22   Completed stick pin.

remember them; we won't recognize the differences. In the rush towards the future, you have to stop in order to see.

I use gold because it doesn't change, because it links us to the past and will bring us into the future. Its properties make an ageless connection. My imagery is from nature because in making connections between all of the life forms, in celebrating their subtleties, I can keep my existence in perspective. I can fit into the pattern of time as it rushes forward.

I dislike having to make a statement about my work; if I felt I could express myself with words, I would leave my images on paper. Words limit and define. A piece is successful if it makes a connection for me and hopefully to the viewer (and wearer), a connection that resists literal intellectualization, something that is primarily a common (universal) feeling.

Mokume: Japanese Lamination

Mokume is an ancient Japanese technique of laminating sheets of different metals and altering the lamination so as to expose the different colored metals in a pattern resembling wood grain. Once the lamination has been made, a number of different techniques can be employed to create the pattern.

One jeweler who has explored this technique in depth is Chuck Evans, professor of jewelry and metalsmithing at Iowa State University. His method is excellent for school or small shop situations. It produces pieces of mokume of a size and density of pattern that is especially suitable for jewelry making. The approach outlined below has almost eliminated the problem, often encountered with this technique, of incomplete soldering of layers.

Materials. 16-gauge metal sheet; jeweler's saw; emery papers; water, toothbrush, and fine pumice powder; borax-base flux; medium or easy solder; torch; soldering pick; pickle; rolling mill; annealing tools; mallet.

Making the Lamination

The lamination is made by soldering together as many as eight layers of 16-gauge metal sheet. The use of heavy-gauge metal helps prevent warping and bending. The different metals, approximately $1^{1}/_{2}''$ (3.8 cm) square, are arranged in layers for color variety and contrast. Many metals can be used, including silver, gold, copper, brass, and bronze. When cutting the squares of metal, use a jeweler's saw rather than shears. The beveled edge left by shears may create problems when soldering.

Now emery the surface of each sheet and clean with clear water, a toothbrush, and fine pumice powder. Paint the clean surfaces with a borax-base flux. Now add solder to the surface of each sheet. Cut five or six $1^{1}/_{4}''$ (3.2 cm) lengths of medium or easy silver solder for each fluxed surface. (Easy solder is used if no further soldering is planned.) Space the solder evenly over the surface, and heat with a torch until it melts. Use the pointed end of a soldering pick to spread the solder. Be certain that the solder covers the entire surface. If spots have been missed, reflux and heat again. Pickle well.

Now each sheet should be flattened to remove the unevenness caused by the solder. Roll each solder-covered square through the rolling mill just enough to smooth the solder surface. The goal here is not to reduce the thickness of the square but rather to create a uniform thickness.

After each piece is rolled, anneal and pickle well. Solder-covered surfaces are cleaned with fine pumice and surfaces without solder

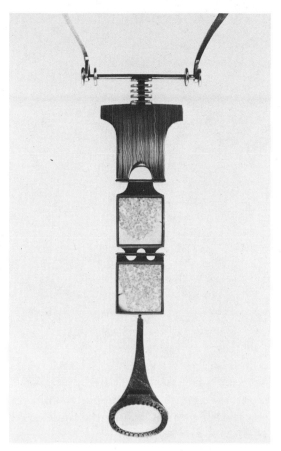

FIG. 6–23 Chuck Evans. Pendant of sterling silver (gold plated), walrus tusk, and moonstone. Constructed, forged neckpiece with multimetal lamination. *Courtesy of the artist.*

FIG. 6–24 Lisa D'Agostino. Pendant of sterling silver, copper, brass, and carnelian. Mokume, in 48 layers. *Courtesy of the artist.*

are emeried. Using a mallet, carefully flatten the metal on a clean anvil. After flattening, clean again with pumice.

To solder the squares together, flux each surface and stack them in the desired order on a flat steel mesh screen placed on top of a tripod soldering stand, as shown in figure 6–18. Heat to melt the solder by alternating the flame from below and above, or use two torches. When the solder flows, apply light pressure with a soldering pick. Hold down the layers until the solder freezes.

Clean with clear water and check for visible gaps between the layers. If more soldering is necessary, reflux and resolder, adding solder where necessary.

Next, run this lamination through a rolling mill until it has been reduced to one-half its thickness. An electric rolling mill, if available, will cut down the work considerably. Anneal whenever the rolling makes the metal work-hardened.

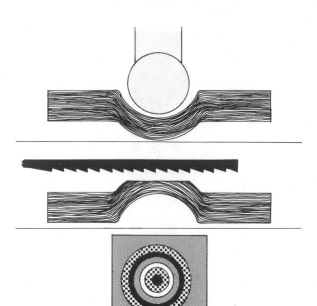

FIG. 6–25   Mokume. After making the lamination, dent the metal (top) and file the dents level with the surface (middle). This will expose the different metals in a pattern (bottom).

To proceed, saw this sheet in half and flatten the two halves with a mallet. The two halves are then soldered together, one on top of the other to double the original number of layers. The cleaning and soldering procedure is the same as explained above. The resulting piece of laminate is, in turn, rolled again through the mill and sawed in half, and the two halves are soldered together. This process is repeated until the desired amount of laminates are made. The pieces shown in figures 6–23 and 6–24 were made with twenty-four and forty-eight layers. The final sheet is rolled out to the gauge desired for the final piece.

Making the Pattern

The wood-grain pattern is made by exposing the underlying layers of metal. The back of the laminated metal is punched in, using repoussé and chasing tools or small dapping punches (see figure 6–25). Different tools will create different effects. These dents in the metal must not be allowed to sink past the center of the sheet or a hole will result when the piece is later filed. The punching can be done with the metal supported in pitch or on a lead block. The procedure for working in pitch is explained on page 60. Clean the metal after removing it from the pitch or lead block.

File the dents in the metal to create a flat sheet (figure 6–25, middle). This filing will expose the different layers of metal and create a wood-grain pattern.

To finish the surface, emery and polish. The metals may be treated with a weak solution of liver of sulfur to accentuate the contrast between the different metals.

Creative Connections

7

Materials can be joined in hundreds of ways. With thought and ingenuity, joinery can be a creative challenge. A jeweler may treat a connection as a minor detail and a necessary distraction. On the other hand, this functional necessity may be the most successful and important part of a piece of jewelry.

DESIGNING YOUR WORK: CREATIVE JOINERY

As designers, we work from a tradition of jewelry making that stretches throughout history, and we also work in a cultural context. No matter how closely we follow tradition, we cannot deny the creative self that lives within us all. It sees things from a unique perspective and awaits expression.

When attacking a problem of joinery, we may delve into this well of experience and find a unique approach to the problem. One need not, however, start from zero. Historical examples of joinery provide a starting point rather than a limitation. Keep an open mind, free from previous conceptions of what a traditional closing looks like. Transfer ideas from one use to another. Many new and unexplored ideas come from daily experience. It may be helpful to make sketches of common objects that use connections. Consider door knobs, plugs, scissors, boxes (hinged or friction fit), refrigerator magnets, folding chairs, zippers, and hair clips. Mechanisms may allow for movement (turning, swinging, stretching, disassembling, or locking), and these provide versatility as to how the piece may be worn. Processes such as sewing, stapling, crimping, and strapping present additional possibilities.

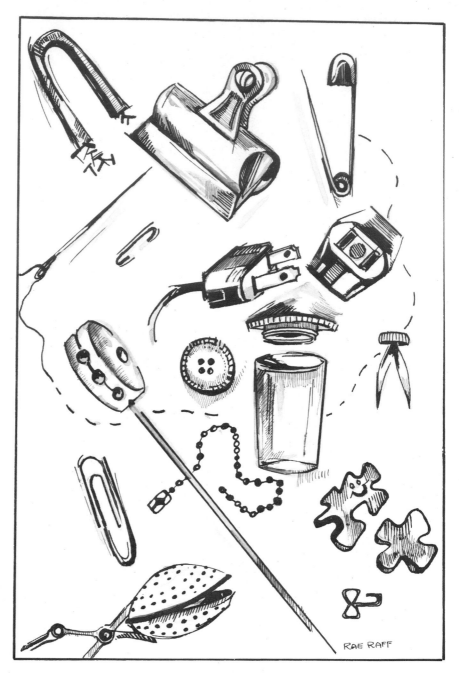

FIG. 7–1   Ideas for creative connections. Drawing by Rae Raff.

Riveting

Riveting is one method of attaching materials without using heat, as in soldering and fusing. Connecting mechanisms that do not require heat in their construction are called cold connections. In riveting, a wire running through the materials is held in place by rivet heads

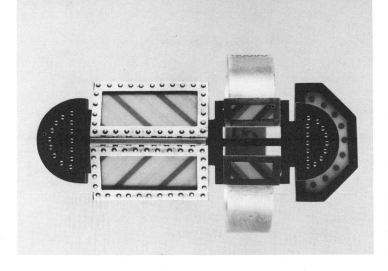

FIG. 7–2   Richard Helzer.
Bracelet of sterling silver,
bronze, and acrylic. This piece
shows the use of rivets to join
materials. *Courtesy of the artist.*

on both ends. Rivets are an excellent means of attaching stone, plastic, bone, wood, and any other materials that cannot be subjected to the high temperatures of the torch flame, yet are strong enough to withstand the hammering necessary to make a rivet. Rivets are also used for their decorative qualities.

Making a Wire Rivet

The rivet is made from a piece of wire or tubing (figure 7–3). Many jewelers use 14-gauge wire for this purpose. Riveting with tubing leaves a hole into which a chain or other material may be threaded.

To make a wire rivet, insert one end of a piece of wire vertically into a smooth-jawed vise to make the first head. Approximately $^1/_{32}''$ (1 mm) of the wire is allowed to protrude above the vise. This protruding wire will be hammered to make a rivet head. To make the head, gently tap the edges of the wire end until it mushrooms and creates an even, rounded head. Do this gradually. When the head has been made, it may be filed into a smooth hemisphere with a needle file, or it may be tapped with a rivet set that has a depression of the proper size.

Next, drill a hole to accept the rivet, using a drill bit of the same diameter as the wire. A tight fit is important. If this hole is too

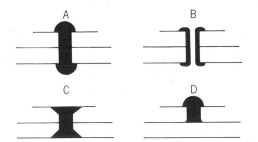

FIG. 7–3   Types of rivets:
(a) raised heads, (b) tube,
(c) countersunk, and
(d) soldered at one end and
raised head at the other end.

large, the rivet wire will bend when hammered and the rivet will not work. If it is too small, it can be made larger using a round needle file.

The rivet is then inserted into the hole and cut off approximately $^1/_{32}''$ (1 mm) from the surface of the materials being riveted. If the wire is cut too long, it will bend when hammered. If it is too short, there will not be enough material to make a large enough head to hold the work together. Before making the second head, file the end of the wire flat. The work is supported on a metal surface plate or in the depression of a hollow punch, dapping block, or rivet set. The second head is spread in the same manner as the first. When the second head is complete, the piece will be securely riveted together.

A single rivet will permit the pieces being joined to swivel around the point of riveting. They will be held stationary if more than one rivet is used. When using more than one rivet on a single piece, complete one rivet before another hole is drilled. This will prevent the holes from becoming misaligned as the rivets are set.

Going a Step Further

Try balling one end of the wire before it is inserted into the drilled hole. Hold the wire vertically into a torch flame and heat the end of the wire until the metal melts into a small ball (figure 7–4). This ball may be used as is or flattened by inserting the wire into a small hole drilled in a metal plate, such as a draw plate, and setting the balled end against the plate. The ball is then flattened slightly with a hammer. The rest of the rivet is completed as explained above.

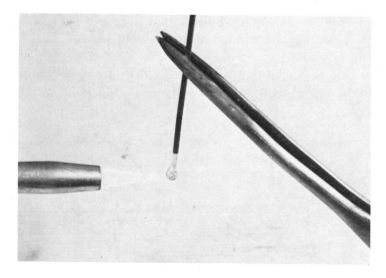

FIG. 7–4   Balling the end of a wire.

FIG. 7–5 Escutcheon pins were used to make the rivets for this pendant. The rivets were set loosely to allow for freedom of movement.

Escutcheon pins can be used for making rivets, as was done for the pendant in figure 7–5. These pins, available at most hardware stores, are made with hemispherical heads. It is therefore necessary to make only one head to complete the rivet.

The ends of the rivet may be countersunk to make them flush with the surface of the metal. This is done by using a cone-shaped burr in the flexible shaft to cut cavities into which the two ends of the rivet may be set. Excess rivet wire which protrudes above the surface of the metal is filed off, leaving a smooth surface. If the rivet is made from the same color metal as the metal being riveted together, the rivet will not be visible (see figure 7–3c).

Try making a rivet in which the wire is first soldered at one end to a sheet of metal (see figure 7–3d). In this way, only one end of the rivet must be set. This method may be used when attaching any material to a metal base.

Try leaving the rivet slightly loose to allow the pieces to swing freely (see figure 7–5).

Plexiglas Rivets

To make a Plexiglas rivet, a fine Plexiglas rod of less than ⅛″ (3 mm) in diameter is used in place of the metal wire. These rivets are not as strong as metal rivets. If the rivets will be subjected to some stress, Plexiglas rivets may be used for decorative effect in conjunction with metal ones. Since no hammering is necessary for making this rivet, it is particularly handy for working in materials that are susceptible to breakage, such as in enameled work.

With a jeweler's saw, cut a rod slightly longer than the thickness of the material into which it is to be inserted. As in making a wire rivet, a hole is drilled with a drill bit of the same diameter as the rod. The Plexiglas rod is held in place within the hole by a ball at each end of the rivet. These balls are made by using a heated nail set, which will melt the Plexiglas rod. The cupped end of the heated nail set is pressed over each end of the rod to form a small ball. (A nail set is a punch-like tool used normally to countersink nails. They come in various sizes.)

The Hinge

The hinge is a mechanism used for joining two straight-edged pieces of metal so that they will swivel around a pin, as shown in the locket in figure 7–6. A hinge is made from thick-walled tubing that is sawed into sections. Alternate sections are soldered to each of the two pieces of metal to be joined. A pin is used to hold the hinge together.

To make a hinge, begin by filing the metals to be joined until they fit closely together. This is accomplished by filing the edges of the metal in a concave shape to correspond to the curve of the tubing (figure 7–7). This will provide a larger surface for soldering and will create a strong joint.

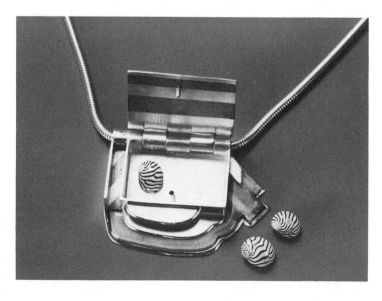

FIG. 7–6   Tom Farrell. "Saturday Morning at the Beach." Locket with hinged cover made from sterling silver, enamel, and copper. *Courtesy of the artist. Photo by Bruce Alter.*

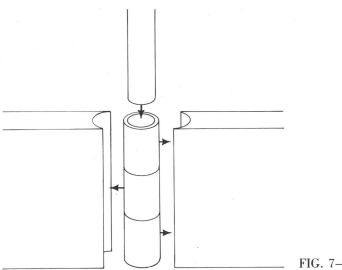

FIG. 7–7   The hinge.

Next, mark off the sections of tubing to be sawed. For most jewelry, three sections are sufficient; however, five or more may be used for added support and large hinges. An odd number of sections will also help to make the hinge strong. When sawing, the tubing may be held in a tube-cutting jig (figure 7–8) in order to saw the edges straight and make the sections equal in size. Sawing may also be done on a bench pin; however, it is difficult to hold the small pieces of tubing and be accurate without using the jig. After sawing, file the ends of the tubing sections flat.

Next, every other section will be soldered to one side of the piece, and the remaining sections are soldered to the other side. Soldering is done on a charcoal block. Care must be taken to align the sections properly in order to make a functioning and well-crafted hinge. A piece of steel wire of the same diameter as the tubing hole is used to hold the sections until they are tacked in place. To accomplish this, insert the wire into the tubing sections, and line them up straight and flat, one against the other.

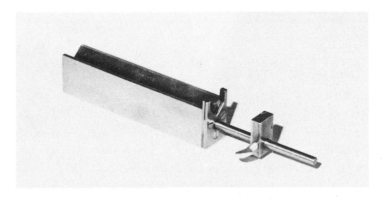

FIG. 7–8   Tube-cutting jig.
Courtesy of Allcraft.

Now the tubing is placed in position between the two pieces of metal to which it will be soldered. One or two paillons of solder are then placed in the center of each of the joints. Check to be certain that you are soldering the correct elements together.

Heat the metal until the solder melts just enough to tack the sections in place. Take care not to overheat the tubing, for it is thin and will melt easily. Do not solder the joints completely at this point or your may end up soldering together more than you want, making the hinge inoperative.

Remove the wire, leaving the sections in place. Separate the two halves of the hinge and complete the soldering, adding solder where needed. If necessary, steel wire, chunks of kiln brick, pumice lumps, or other propping devices may be used to hold the tubing in place against the metal.

To join the sections after soldering, a pin slightly longer than the hinge is inserted into the tubing so that the sections are held together in their proper position. To hold the pin permanently in place, the ends are mushroomed using a chasing or riveting hammer, setting one end of the pin against a steel surface and spreading the other end. Work on one side at a time until the hinge is tightly fitted together. (See *Riveting* for instructions on how to set the pin.)

Hinge Variations

To use a hinge as a closing device, solder the tubing sections in place as described above. The pin, rather than made stationary, is left free so that it may be removed in order to open the catch. A loop is made on the top of the pin and is attached to a chain, which holds the pin to the rest of the piece and prevents it from getting lost. The loop also keeps the pin from sliding out. The pin is inserted into the hinge with the loop on top so that gravity will help to keep it in place.

A simple hinge may be made by soldering a solid strip of tubing to one of the two pieces of metal to be joined. A wire is placed through the tubing, and each end of the wire is soldered to the second piece of metal.

Nuts, Bolts, and Screws

Nuts and bolts are a simple and decorative means of joining materials. They are screwed together with the bolt first passing through the materials to be joined. This type of joinery has the advantage of easy disassembly for repair. A versatile piece may be made by creating removable or interchangeable sections, which may be screwed on, moved to a different part of the piece, or removed entirely (figure 7–9a and b).

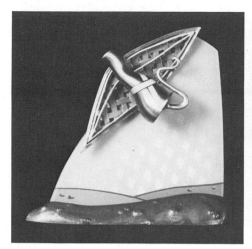
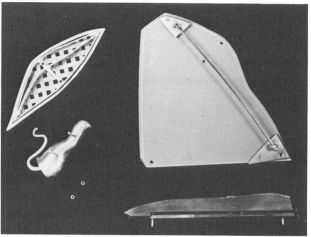

FIG. 7–9a Bruce Metcalf. "Bright Figure over a Low, Bad Land." Pin of brass, sterling silver, copper, plastics, and paint. View with parts screwed together. *Courtesy of the artist.*

FIG. 7–9b View with parts separated by unscrewing nuts.

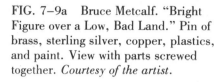

Nuts and bolts may be made by the jeweler or purchased ready-made. Tiny brass nuts and bolts may be purchased from J. I. Morris Company (see *Sources of Supplies*).

Nuts and bolts may be handmade by using a tap and die set to cut the threads.

These sets, available at jewelry supply houses, come in a variety of sizes for making different size threaded holes and posts. The tap is used to make the threaded hole into which the threaded post will be screwed. The die is used to thread the post.

To make the threaded hole, the metal must be thick enough to cut a minimum of three threads; the screw will not work with fewer threads. Hold the metal firmly in a vise and drill a hole slightly smaller than the inside diameter of the threads of the tap. Next, make the threads by turning the tap, held in a tap holder or screw chuck, clockwise into the drilled hole. A drop of oil will lubricate the tap while cutting.

Be certain to hold the tap perpendicular to the metal. Do the cutting gradually, making only two turns at a time and then backing out to remove the metal cuttings. Use the tap carefully, for it is brittle and can easily be broken.

The threaded post is made by using the die corresponding in number to the tap. This will give you the correct size bolt to match the hole that you have just cut. The wire, rod, or tubing used to make the bolt must be slightly larger in diameter than the outside diameter of the tap thread. Hold the wire firmly in a vise in a vertical position. Cut the post threads in a clockwise direction using the die. Lubricate the die with oil while cutting.

Links and Chains

Although a great variety of commercial chains are available, you may want to make your own chain. A handcrafted chain may be made to complement the design of your piece or as a work of art on its own right.

Making Jump Rings

To make your own jump rings for a chain or for linking materials together, wire is first wound tightly around a rod or dowel of the required diameter. This may be done by hand or by inserting the rod into the chuck of a drill and turning the drill to coil the wire. Make the coil about 1″ (2.5 cm) long, or make a longer coil and cut it into 1″ (2.5 cm) pieces for easy handling. The coil is removed from the rod and sawed into links with a jeweler's saw.

To saw the links, hold the coil in a vise and insert the sawblade into the coil. Now, saw downward until you have cut your way out of the coil and the links separate (figure 7–10).

Two Simple Chains

A simple chain may be made by soldering links into one another. To solder thin wire, use a small torch tip and a low flame aimed away from the other links. Half of the links are soldered closed (figure 7–11), and the other half are used to join the links into a chain (figure 7–12). In this way, as few links as possible are soldered while attached, thus minimizing the chance of melting the links. Links of various sizes and shapes may be joined together to create a unique chain. The links may be forged flat with a small

FIG. 7–10   To make jump rings, insert the saw blade into the coiled wire and saw downward until the rings separate.

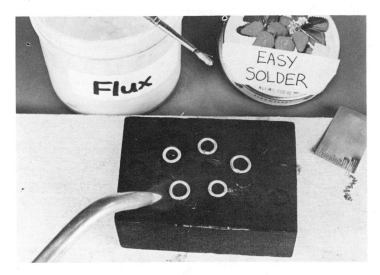

FIG. 7–11   Solder half of the rings closed.

FIG. 7–12   Solder the remaining half of the rings closed after inserting them through two soldered rings. A "third hand" was used to hold the rings for soldering.

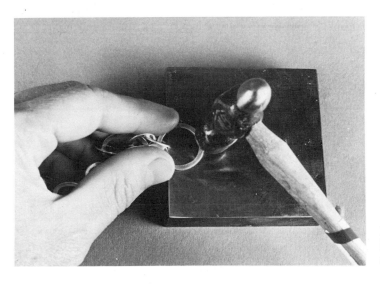

FIG. 7–13   Use a small ball-peen hammer to forge the rings flat.

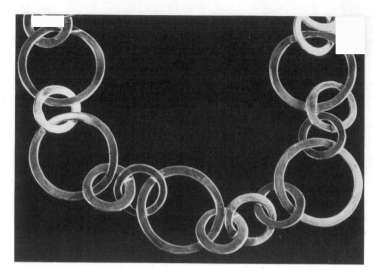

FIG. 7–14   The finished chain.

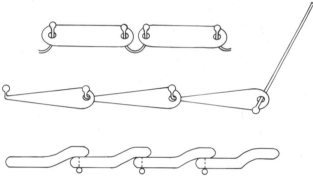

FIG. 7–15   Three chains.

ball-peen hammer (figure 7–13). The finished chain is shown in figure 7–14.

Another simple chain is made by cutting 1 ¼" (3.2 cm) lengths of 14-gauge (or thicker) round wire. Ball one end of each wire by heating it with a torch (see figure 7–4). Next, making one link at a time, forge the other end of the wire flat until it is wide enough to accept a drilled hole. Drill a hole just large enough to fit the 14-gauge wire. Slip a second wire into the hole and forge the unballed end flat. This will hold the links together. Next, drill a hole in this link and continue the process until the chain is of the desired length (figure 7–15, middle). A hook may be added to close the chain (see figure 7–26).

Gallery of Connecting Mechanisms

The following are a number of solutions that jewelers have arrived at to solve the design and functional aspects of connecting jewelry forms together or to the wearer.

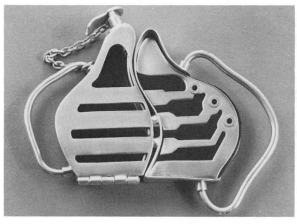

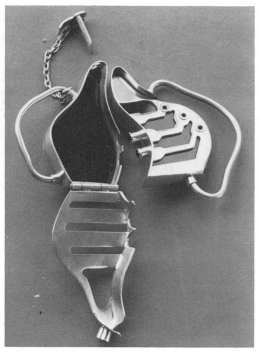

FIG. 7–16a   Barbara Mail. Belt buckle of sterling silver, Plexiglas, and synthetic garnet. Closed view. *Courtesy of the artist.*

FIG. 7–16b   Open view.

FIG. 7–17   Adine Kaufman. Hinged bracelet with tension clip. The hinge is at bottom center; the clip is on the right. *Courtesy of the artist.*

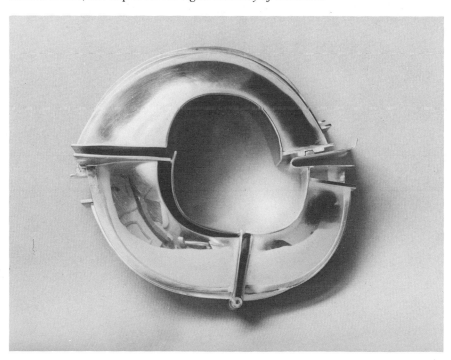

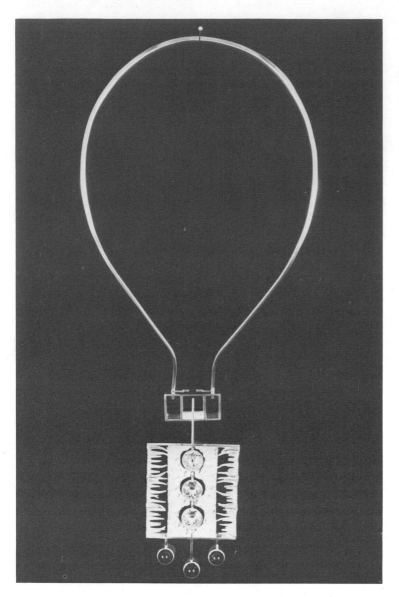

FIG. 7–18a   Carey Smith. Neckpiece with maze clasp, of sterling silver, amethyst, and black onyx. Forged, fabricated, and cast. 1969. *Courtesy of the artist.*

FIG. 7–18b   Maze catch. The wires are squeezed together to enter the center chamber. Tension forces them into the outer chambers.

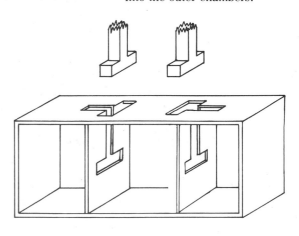

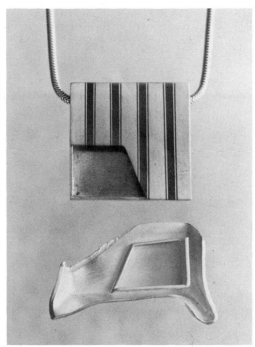

FIG. 7–19a   Tom Farrell. "Bed Box." Locket of sterling silver and copper. Closed view. Friction-fit closing. *Courtesy of the artist.*

FIG. 7–19b   Open view.

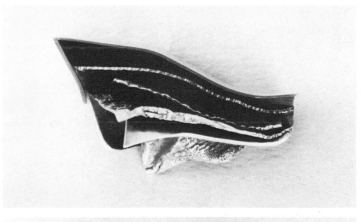

FIG. 7–20a   Tom Farrell. Pin of silver. Reticulated. Front view. *Courtesy of the artist.*

FIG. 7–20b   Back view. Pin stem and hook are an integral part of the design.

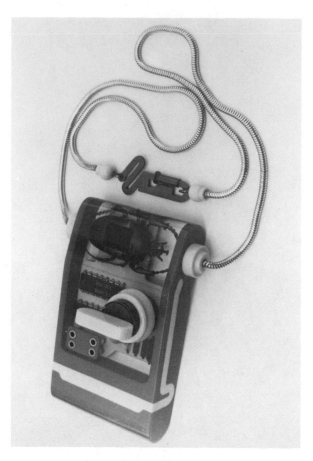

FIG. 7–21a   Bob Natalini. Pendant with spring clasp, of polyester, sterling silver, tropical beetle, and functioning electronics (beetle has a light matrix in its body that goes through a long sequence of patterns). 1977. *Courtesy of the artist.*

FIG. 7–21b   Spring clasp. The cylinder containing the spring slides back to create an opening, and then the jump ring is slid off.

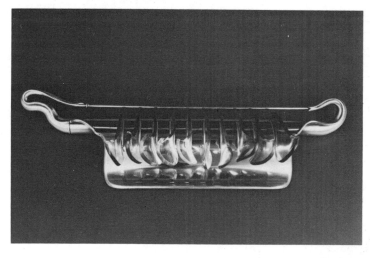

FIG. 7–22a   Ronna Silver. "Sliding Brooch." Sterling silver and acrylic. Closed view. *Photo by Ronna Silver.*

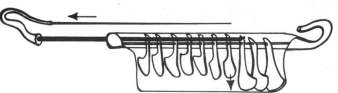

FIG. 7–22b   When the pin stem is slid open, the acrylic segments, which pivot on a rod, drop down upon the polished background. When the pin is slid back into place, a form slides over the short ends of the segments, pushes them down, and causes the segments to rise one by one back into position.

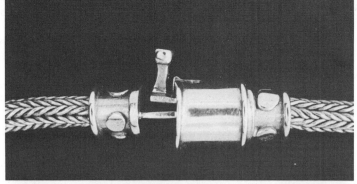

FIG. 7–23a   Carol Steen. Partially closed catch. *Courtesy of the artist. Photo by D. James Dee.*

FIG. 7–23b   Open catch. The tongue is depressed to enter the groove; when released, pressure on the roof of the groove prevents the clasp from opening.

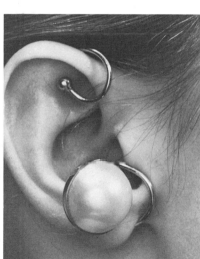

FIG. 7–24a   Sigurd Persson. Ear jewel of gold with pearl. 1964. *Courtesy of the artist.*

FIG. 7–24b   Ear jewel of silver. 1964.

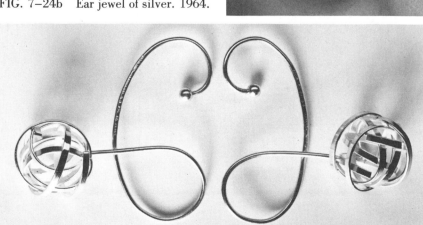

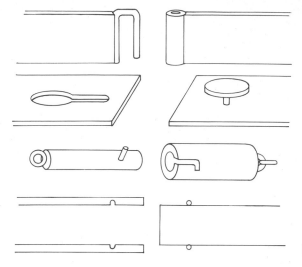

FIG. 7–25   Four closings.

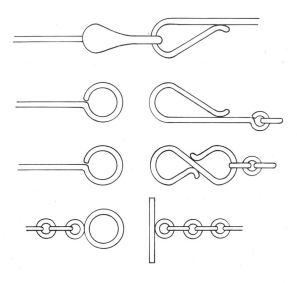

FIG. 7–26   Four hook closings.

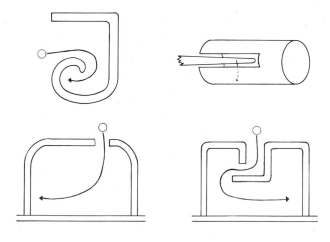

FIG. 7–27   Four pin catches, which catch a pin stem as in a safety pin.

Jewelry Settings

8

Stones and other nonmetals are valued for their color, rarity, size, brilliance, and durability. In a piece of jewelry, they enhance the design by adding elements of color, texture, contrast, and luster. Stones may be used in the rough, or they may be carved, tumbled, inlayed, or cut and polished.

Other materials such as pearls, wood, bone, plastic, fossils, and found objects can be set in a piece of jewelry through any number of methods. They are usually secured in a setting that supports them from below and clamps them from above. Any settings that hold a stone securely and display it to best advantage may be used. There is a great deal of room here for creativity, and you should not feel constricted by conventional methods.

The strength, transparency, and shape of the material, as well as the design of the work, are taken into account when choosing the setting. Consider how light will enter the stone, whether fragile materials are adequately protected, and whether the different materials are displayed harmoniously.

Knowledge of where a gemstone falls on the Mohs scale of hardness is helpful in determining how to set a gem. The Mohs scale measures the relative ease with which one stone can be scratched by another (see page 209). The scale runs from 1 to 10, with 10 being the hardest known substance, the diamond. Note that a hard stone may not necessarily be tough: A hard stone may resist scratching, but then it may be easily shattered when struck against a hard surface. Materials that are below 7 on the Mohs scale should be set in a sheltered spot in jewelry that may be scratched. Consider where and when the jewelry is to be worn. A soft stone in a necklace need not be as well protected as it would in a ring, for example.

FIG. 8–1   Gorget, or plate of necklet. Gold and jewels.Tibetan XVII–XIX.
The Metropolitan Museum of Art, Kennedy Fund, 1915.

The size of a stone often determines how it is set. Some settings
are more suited to small stones, while others work best with larger
stones. The unit of weight of a gem is the *carat*. One carat is equal
to .2 grams (200 milligrams). This unit of measurement is different
from the *karat* used to measure the fineness of gold. The parts of a
gemstone are illustrated in figure 8–3.

Bezel Setting: Making a Pendant

The bezel setting is most often used to mount a cabochon or an
irregularly shaped stone with a flat bottom (figures 8–4, 8–5, and
8–8). It is constructed from flat wire, which surrounds and is

FIG. 8–2   Sigurd Persson. Necklet of gold and pearls. 1963. *Courtesy of the
artist*.

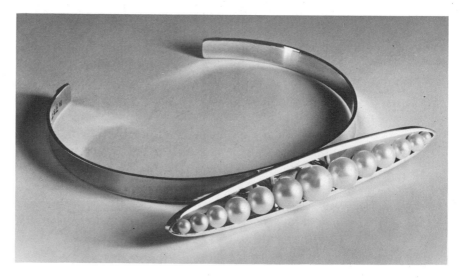

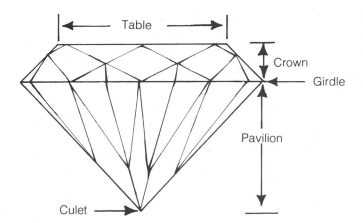

FIG. 8–3   Parts of a faceted stone.

compressed over the stone in order to hold it against a base. A bezel is most often made from soft metal such as fine silver, which can be easily pushed over the stone for setting. The thickness of most bezel wire is 26 to 28 gauge. A good bezel height will allow the stone to be gripped tightly yet allow as much of the stone to be seen as possible. If too much bezel extends over the stone, it may become crimped when the stone is set.

Materials.   18- or 20-gauge sheet metal; bezel wire; $1/4''$ (6 mm) piece of $3/32''$ (2 mm) tubing; cabochon; chain for the pendant; pencil or scribe; bezel mandrel; wooden or rawhide mallet; hard, medium, and easy solder; needle files; Scotch stone or rifle files; thin wire; stone pusher or rocker; masking tape; flat and polished chasing tool; chasing hammer; burnisher; soldering, pickling and polishing materials.

FIG. 8–4   Sigurd Persson. Necklace with stones set in bezels. 1965. *Courtesy of the artist.*

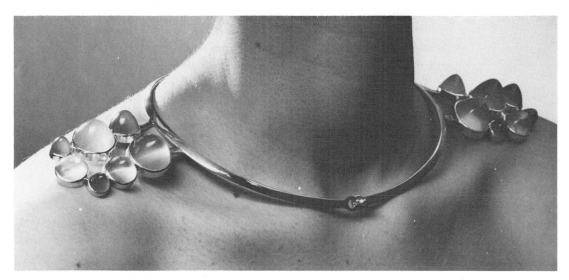

FIG. 8–5 Mary Ann Scherr. Necklace of walrus tusk, black coral, jade, ebony, 14K gold, sterling silver, and opals. The opals are set in bezels. *Courtesy of the artist.*

Making the Bezel

The bezel wire may be wrapped directly around the base of the stone to determine the length of the bezel (figure 8–7). Extra length is added to allow for filing the ends square. The perimeter of the stone may also be measured by wrapping a piece of thin wire, such as binding wire, around the base of the stone. The wire is twisted tightly where the two ends meet and then removed from the stone and the twist cut off, leaving a length of wire the exact measurement of the stone. This wire is straightened and its length marked on the bezel wire, with a small allowance added for filing the ends of the bezel wire square. After marking the desired length with a pencil or scribe, the bezel wire is cut with bezel shears. The ends of the wire are squared with a flat needle file. The fit around the stone should be checked before proceeding.

To solder the bezel wire closed, spring the ends together so they meet squarely (see figure 2–20). When setting a rectangular stone, be certain that the seam is not on a corner. Next, flux, and solder the seam using hard solder (figure 8–9). Very little solder is needed. In order to control the amount of solder, use paillons or

FIG. 8–6 Barbara Stanger. "Jerusalem."
Ceremonial wedding ring. Sterling silver, tourmaline,
amethysts, and onyx beads. Cabochons are bezel set.
Courtesy of the artist. Photo by Ralph Heigl.

snipped wire solder rather than soldering directly off a coil of wire solder. A small torch tip and low flame will prevent the bezel from melting. Remember that the solder will flow toward the heat. Use a pick if necessary to coax the solder over the seam. Use a flat needle file to file off excess solder so that the seam is no longer visible.

Fitting the Bezel

If the bezel is slightly small for the stone, it may be stretched by gently forcing it down the taper of the bezel mandrel with a wooden mallet. If the bezel is too large, it must be remade. For a smooth, even bezel, the fit must be exact. To remove kinks in the bezel, use a mallet to gently tap the wire around a mandrel. The bottom edge of the bezel is made flat by rubbing it against a piece of emery

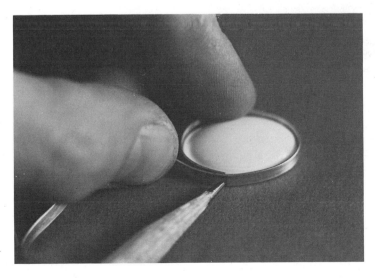

FIG. 8–7 Measure the bezel
around the stone and mark the
length with a pencil.

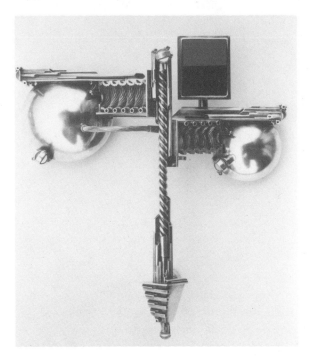

FIG. 8–8   Richard Mawdsley. Pin of sterling silver and black onyx. The stone is set in a bezel. *Courtesy of the artist.*

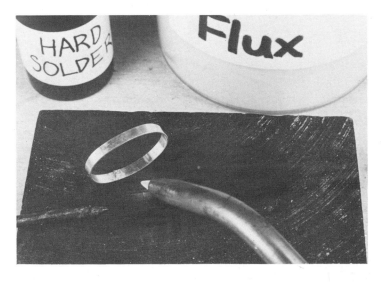

FIG. 8–9   Solder the bezel ends together with hard solder.

paper supported on a flat surface (figure 8–10). Next, fit the bezel around the stone for reshaping before soldering it to the base.

If the bezel is going to be soldered onto a curved surface, such as a ring shank, the bottom edge of the bezel is filed to fit the contour of the base (see figure 8–11b). Any gaps will make soldering difficult, if not impossible. A strip of square or rectangular wire may be soldered along the inside perimeter of the bezel for support (figure 8–11a and b).

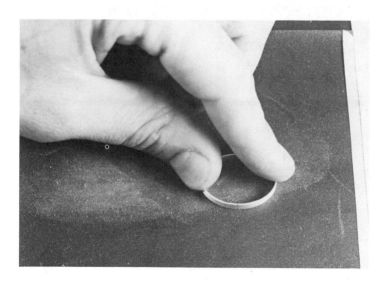

FIG. 8–10   Emery the bottom edge of the bezel flat.

Soldering the Bezel to the Base

Cut the sheet metal to the desired shape for the base. To solder the bezel onto the base, place the base with the bezel in place on a tripod. Flux the piece. Place paillons of medium solder along the inside seam where the bezel joins the base. Heat the work *mainly from below* until the solder flows along the entire seam (figure 8–12). A pick may be used to help the solder flow. When the solder flows, remove the torch immediately. Take care not to overheat, for it is easy to melt a bezel. Next, pickle the piece. If the proper amount of solder is used, no cleanup is necessary. Remove any excess solder with a scraper (a tool with three sharp edges) Use a needle or rifle file or Scotch stone to smooth the area further.

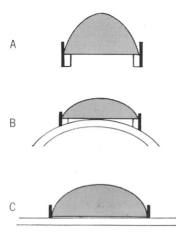

A

B

C

FIG. 8–11   Bezel settings. (a) The stone is seated on a bearing rather than a solid sheet in order to reduce the weight and allow light to enter. A bezel (solid black) holds the stone on the bearing. (b) The bezel and bearing are filed to fit the contour of a curved surface. (c) A simple bezel is soldered to a background sheet.

FIG. 8–12   Solder the bezel onto the backing with medium solder. Apply heat mainly from below.

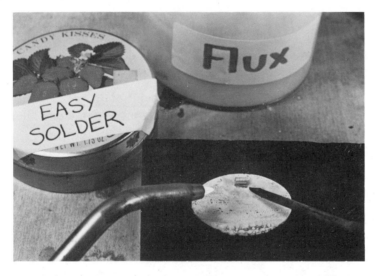

FIG. 8–13   Solder the tubing on with easy solder.

FIG. 8–14   The stone may be raised within the bezel with a wire that has been bent into a flat spiral.

Finishing

In order to hang the pendant from a chain, a ¼″ (6 mm) length of ³/₃₂″ (2 mm) diameter tubing is soldered to the back with easy solder (figure 8–13). Be certain to center the tubing or the piece will not hang straight.

Now the bezel is filed to the proper height. A stone may be raised within the bezel using sawdust or thin wire. If wire is used, it is wound into a flat spiral and then inserted into the bezel cup (figure 8–14).

Before setting the stone, the entire piece is finished. Polishing is completed before setting the stone to decrease the likelihood of damaging it.

Setting the Stone

Place the stone squarely into the setting and begin to push the bezel over the stone to secure it. A stone pusher, or rocker, is used for this purpose (figure 8–15). To distribute the bezel evenly over the stone, the metal is pushed down gradually. First push gently on one side, then on the opposite side, and then proceed to the other two sides (figure 8–16). When pushing the bezel over an angular stone, push down the corners first. Alternating sides will keep the stone centered and the metal evenly distributed. Continue pushing in this manner until the entire bezel is flat against the stone.

If necessary, gently file and emery to remove tool marks or uneven areas. This must be done sparingly, since the bezel is thin. A chasing tool tapped gently with a hammer may be used to tighten the bezel. Burnish the bezel around the stone. Masking tape may be used to protect the metal of the base from being scratched (figure 8–17). The piece may be completed by polishing on a machine or by hand. Tape also may be used to protect the stone during polishing. The completed pendant is shown in figure 8–18.

Bezel Variations

Try using twisted wire soldered around the bezel for a decorative effect. Or alter the shape of the strip of bezel wire by cutting into the top edge to form scallops, points, or other patterns. Try using a bezel that does not completely surround the stone, yet catches it securely. If sheet metal has been used as a backing, a hole may be sawed in the sheet to allow light to enter the stone from below and lighten the piece. Another method of allowing light to enter from the back is to solder a square or rectangular piece of wire along the inside perimeter of the bezel wire, rather than soldering the bezel to a solid sheet, as shown in figure 8–11a.

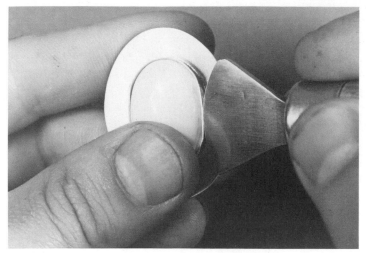

FIG. 8–15   Push the bezel over the stone with a rocker.

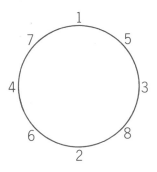

FIG. 8–16   The numbers indicate the order in which to push the sides of the bezel over the stone.

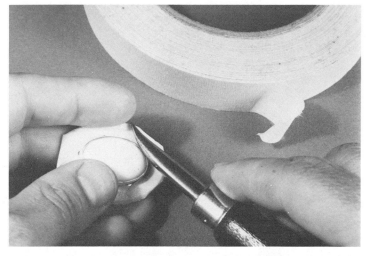

FIG. 8–17   Smooth the bezel over the stone with a burnisher.

FIG. 8–18   Completed pendant with ivory in a bezel setting.

Tube Setting

A variation on the bezel setting is the tube setting, which is used to set small, round cabochons or faceted stones, as shown in figures 8–19 and 8–20. The tubing may be made or bought to fit the stone. The tubing wall must be thick enough to allow for the seat to be cut and the rim to be pushed over the stone. The correct tube size is determined by fitting the stone so that it rests on the tubing wall. There should be enough of the wall beneath it to support the stone and enough extending beyond the stone to push over it for setting (figure 8–21).

The tubing is soldered in place before cutting the seat for the stone. The seat is cut with a setting bur held in a flexible shaft. The size of the bur should match the diameter of the stone. This measurement is taken using a caliper, divider, or gauge (see figure 8–22). Drill the seat deep enough to recess the stone so that the girdle of the stone lies just below the top of the tube. This will create a seat for the stone and will thin the outer wall slightly so that it may be easily pushed over the stone. Do not drill deeper than necessary because the edge may become too thin and crack when it is pushed over the stone.

After the entire piece is completed and polished, the stone is dropped into the seat and the metal rim pushed over the stone with a cupped burnishing tool in a size that fits over the stone. It is sometimes helpful to use a small amount of epoxy to hold the stone in place while pushing the rim over the stone.

Gypsy Setting

The gypsy setting is similar to the tube setting except that the seat is drilled directly into the metal rather than into a tube. The metal must be thick enough to provide the depth needed to house the stone. It may be thickened where the stone is to be set by soldering on an additional sheet of metal. Cast pieces may also be made thick enough for this setting.

First, drill a narrow hole through the metal to serve as a guide for the setting bur. Using a setting bur of the same diameter as the girdle of the stone, drill a seat for the stone so that the girdle lies just below the surface of the metal (figure 8–23). Next, carve a groove with a file or graver around the hole about $1/16''$ (2 mm) from the edge. This creates a ring of metal that will later be pushed over the stone to hold it against the seat (see figure 8-23c). Push the rim over the stone by hammering it with a flat chasing tool or stone pusher. The metal around the stone is then filed smooth, emeried, and polished. After filing, the mechanics of this setting should not be visible.

FIG. 8–19 Tom Farrell. Pendant of sterling silver, tourmalines, and enamel. The stones are set in tubes. *Courtesy of the artist. Photo by Bruce Alter.*

FIG. 8–20 Sigurd Persson. Bracelet of white gold and diamonds. 1963. *Courtesy of the artist.*

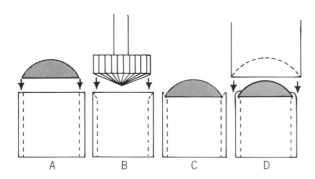

FIG. 8–21 Tube setting. (a) Choose a stone and tube that fit so that the stone rests between the inner and outer edge of the tube. (b) Use a bur to cut a seat for the stone. (c) Insert the stone and (d) push the thinned wall over the stone with a cupped burnishing tool.

For stones with a deep pavilion, a bur with a taper corresponding in shape to the stone is used to cut the seat. The drilled hole may be enlarged to allow for the depth of a stone. This is done from the underside of the setting with a flat bur.

Paved Setting (Pavé)

The paved setting is used to set many small stones close to each other, creating a stone-paved effect with almost no metal showing, as in figure 8–24. Small cabochons and faceted stones may be set in this way. The seat is made as in gypsy setting, but the stone is held in place by small beads rather than a ring of metal. The beads are raised from the metal surrounding the stone using a pointed graver which cuts deeper as it approaches the stone. The resulting bur is then formed into a bead using a beading tool of the correct

FIG. 8–22 Tools for tube setting: gauge, setting burs, and burnishing tools. *Courtesy of Allcraft.*

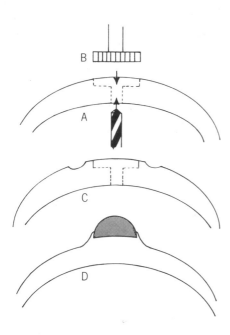

FIG. 8–23 Gypsy setting. (a) Drill a hole to act as a guide for the bur. (b) Cut a seat for the stone with a bur. (c) Carve a groove about $^1/_{16}''$ (2 mm) from the edge of the hole. (d) Insert the stone and push the remaining ring of metal around the stone.

size. These beads will hold the stone against the metal. The small grooves left by the graver will be visible in the finished piece.

Prong Settings

The prong setting, which may be used for any type of stone, is most often used to set faceted stones. Prongs are spaced at intervals rather than totally surrounding the stone, allowing light to enter

FIG. 8–24 Sigurd Persson. Ring of white gold and diamonds, paved setting. Collection of Goldsmiths' Hall, London.

from many angles. This adds life to a translucent or transparent stone and also permits more of the stone to be seen, as illustrated in figure 8–25.

A minimum of three prongs is necessary to secure a stone, but in most cases, four or more prongs are used. The prong must be strong enough to hold the stone firmly over the small area it grabs, so it must be made from stronger and thicker metal than the bezel. For this reason, fine silver and other soft metals are not used.

Prong Settings for a Cabochon

In order to prong set a flat-bottomed stone such as a cabochon, wire prongs are soldered at right angles to a background sheet (figure 8–26a). Round, half-round, or rectangular wire may be used to make the prongs. When soldering, hold the prongs with tweezers or a third hand.

Flux the sheet of metal and the prongs. To solder, heat the prong and let the solder flow onto the end of it. Then heat the sheet to a point just below the temperature at which the solder will flow. Handy Flux is a good indicator because it becomes clear at this temperature. Immediately, the prong is held in place on the preheated sheet, and the joint between the prong and sheet is heated until the solder flows. The solder will flow very soon because the small prong quickly heats to soldering temperature. This prevents the prong from melting as a result of the great difference in size between the metals.

When soldering subsequent prongs, direct the torch flame away from the previously soldered prongs. Some jewelers find it helpful to

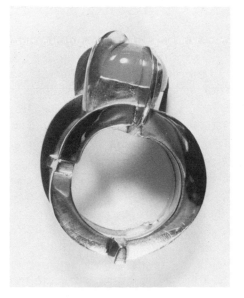

FIG. 8–25 Adine Kaufman. Ring of sterling silver and chrysoprase. Prong setting. *Courtesy of the artist.*

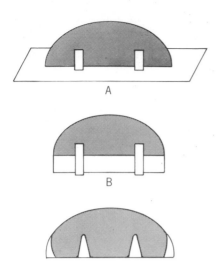

FIG. 8–26 Prong settings for a cabochon. (a) The prongs are soldered to a background sheet. (b) The prongs are soldered to the outer edge of a bezel. (c) The prongs and base are cut from a single sheet of metal.

coat soldered joints with yellow ochre to protect them from reflowing. Yellow ochre is mixed with water and applied with a small brush.

After the prongs are soldered in place, cut and file them to the correct length and shape. The ends of the prongs may be thinned with a file. This will make bending over a sharp curve easier, and it will enable the prongs to lie flat against the stone. After the piece is emeried and polished, the stone is inserted for setting. To set the stone, the prongs are gradually pushed down with a stone pusher or burnisher until they lie flush with the stone.

Prong-Setting Variations

One type of prong setting is made by soldering prongs to the outside of a bezel (figure 8–26b).

Cabochons may also be set by locking the stone against a tapered hole in the metal and holding it in place with prongs. In this type of setting, the prongs are soldered onto the underside of the metal and they are not seen from the top of the piece. To make this setting, cut a hole smaller than the stone's base into the sheet of the metal. Then taper the hole with a needle file so that it fits the contour of the stone and the stone can be held snugly in place, with its bottom flush with the bottom of the sheet metal. The taper should narrow toward the top of the hole. The prongs are soldered at right angles onto the underside of the metal close to, but not touching, the edge of the tapered hole. After filing, emerying, and polishing the piece, the stone is inserted from the bottom and the prongs pushed up to hold the stone firmly against the metal (figure 8–27).

Another prong setting for flat-bottomed stones may be cut from a single sheet of metal (see figure 8–26c). First trace and score the

FIG. 8–27 Prong setting for a cabochon. After a hole is drilled and tapered to hold the stone, prongs are soldered onto the underside of the metal. The stone is locked against the metal with the prongs.

outline of the stone onto the metal. Then score a second line around this first shape. The distance between the two lines is equal to the length of the prongs. The prongs are then scored on the metal. Saw out the outline of the stone and prongs with a jeweler's saw and refine the shape with needle files. Before bending the prongs up to a 90°-angle, score the lines along the bend two-thirds of the way down using a triangular file, graver, or scoring tool. This will help to make the bend crisp and accurate. For added strength, flow solder into the scored line after it has been bent to a 90°-angle.

After emerying and polishing the piece, insert the stone. Bend the prongs over the stone until they lie flush against it. The setting may be used alone as a pendant or soldered onto another sheet.

Prong Settings for a Faceted Stone

A prong setting for a faceted stone is constructed so that the stone is held by the prongs at its girdle (the widest point of the stone). A notch is made in the prongs where they meet the girdle in order to support it from below and clamp it from above. The notch is cut into the prongs using a needle file or a hart bur held in the flexible shaft (figure 8–28). After finishing the piece and inserting the stone, the prongs are pushed over the stone and filed to a taper. A burnisher is used to push the prongs flat against the stone so they will not catch onto clothing.

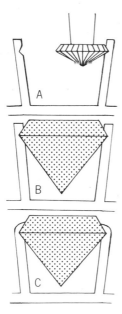

FIG. 8–28 Prong setting for a faceted stone. (a) Cut a notch in the prongs to hold the girdle of the stone. (b) Insert the stone in the notch. (c) Push the prongs over the stone. The prongs may be filed to allow them to lie flat against the stone.

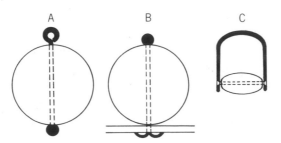

FIG. 8–29   Three ways to set a bead. (a) Ball one end of a wire, thread the bead, and bend a hook. (b) Split one end of a wire and ball the other end. Thread the wire through the bead and metal and spread the split end to fasten the bead in place. (c) Rivet a bead between two pieces of metal.

Setting a Bead

A stone with a hole running through it may be set against a sheet of metal with a piece of wire that has a head on one end and is split at the other end (figure 8–29b). Use a piece of wire the same diameter as the hole in the stone and approximately $^1/_4''$ (6 mm) longer than the stone and metal through which it will be inserted. Drill a hole the same diameter as the wire into the metal where the stone is to be set. The head on the wire is made by balling the wire, using a torch (see figure 7–4), or by spreading the wire with a hammer, as when making a rivet (see page 125). The wire is then inserted through the hole in the stone and metal. The end is split with a jeweler's saw. The split end is spread apart to secure the stone in place.

Figure 8–29c suggests a simple bead ring. The shank of the ring is a section of wire bent to a U shape. Holes are drilled at each end of the U to accept the wire on which a bead will be strung. The ends of the wire are riveted in place.

Materials and Methods: Taking Another Look

9

Contemporary jewelers are increasingly appreciative of the variety of available materials. No longer are silver, gold, platinum, and precious gems the only materials used in making fine jewelry. Anything and everything is now in the domain of the jeweler, giving contemporary jewelry more diversity and bringing a new excitement to the work.

This change in attitude has been brought about by many factors. The jewelry of other cultures, such as Native American and African jewelry, is now more accessible, and it has taught us to appreciate materials that we have previously ignored: seeds, clay, cord, shells, and wood, for example.

People are also acutely aware of the importance of ecology in today's world. Many have come to respect and value the notion of recycling materials. Old forks are being turned into bracelets, and dented silver, pewter bowls, vases, and broken jewelry into new jewelry. Wire from an old motor, pieces from a wooden bowl, lenses from eyeglasses, old photos—all are being recycled. These materials often incorporate their "ready-made" textures and designs into the new piece. A new dimension is added when an old material is placed in a new context. It brings with it a history from a former life. Many jewelers frequent junk stores, flea markets, garage sales, and hardware stores, always keeping an eye out, taking a new look at old materials. If you are lucky, you may find old billiard balls, buttons, and knife handles made of bone, ivory, and shell.

The increased cost of precious metals and stones has also led people to explore other materials. Expensive materials are still used but often in smaller quantity.

You may discover materials that have never before been used in

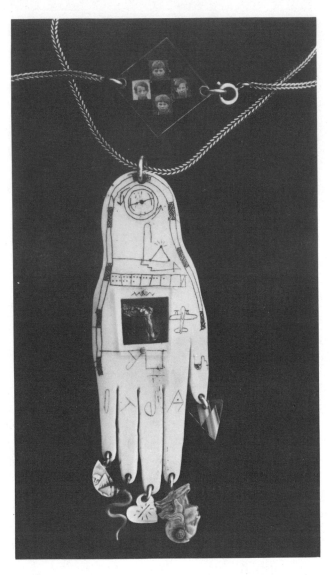

FIG. 9–1   Bob Natalini. Scrimshaw and mixed media. *Courtesy of the artist.*

jewelry. Here are a few ideas to get you thinking: parts of musical instruments, such as ebony or ivory from an old piano; toy and watch parts; fabric, yarn, and leather scraps; hardware, such as washers and brads; bits of broken bottles, mirrors, and beach glass; samples of materials such as Plexiglas; soup bones; shells; clay; feathers; coins; bugs; seeds; nuts; broken, hand-painted china; keys; printer's letters.

Not only is the spectrum of materials available to the jeweler broadening, but the processes used are expanding. With the recent surge of interest in crafts, jewelers are coming into contact with weaving, blacksmithing, glassblowing, ceramics, photography. Craftspeople are coming together in schools, workshops, communities, crafts organizations, and exhibitions, and they are communicating and learning from one another.

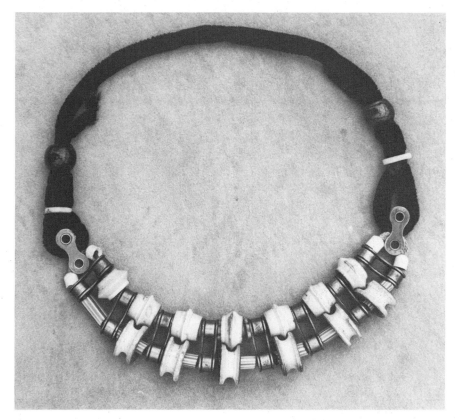

FIG. 9–2 Van LeBus. Necklace of porcelain insulators, bicycle-chain links, glass beads, and velvet cord. 1976. *Courtesy of the artist. Photo by Bob Natalini.*

FIG. 9–3 Three strands of hair with gold hook. American. *The Metropolitan Museum of Art. Gift of John A. de Cesare, 1974.*

Plastics in Jewelry

Plastic is a relatively new material, and only recently have artists been experimenting and discovering how to work with its unique qualities. It was first discovered in 1869 but was not used industrially until 1909. In the past, plastic has been used mainly to mimic other materials, such as wood and glass. Today, there are many different plastics, and each has its own characteristics, which can be exploited for its own sake. New plastics and new applications are continuously being made available to the jeweler.

Plastics can be manufactured to combine many properties, including hardness, elasticity, clarity, durability, and resistance to heat and cold. They can be poured, bent, vacuum formed, sawed, drilled, laminated, filed, carved, and colored. They come in virtually any form—sheet, rod, tube, foam, film, woven cloth, and liquid—and can be transparent, translucent, or opaque. Working in plastics, like enameling, enables the jeweler to incorporate a wide range of colors in a piece.

The two major classifications of plastics are thermoplastic and thermosetting. Thermoplastics, such as acrylic (under such brand names as Plexiglas, Lucite, Perspex, and Acryloid), polycarbonate (such as Lexan), and polystyrene, are solid at room temperature and can be softened by heat and shaped. When allowed to cool, they will retain the new shape. If reheated, they will return to their original shape, making errors easy to correct. Because of this property, thermoplastics are said to have a "memory."

Thermosetting plastics, such as epoxy and polyester resin, on the other hand, will not reliquify with the application of heat. They will remain solid until they reach the temperature at which they decompose. Usually liquid at room temperature, they harden with the application of heat or a catalyst. Once they cure, they cannot return to their original state.

The general characteristics of epoxies and resins are outlined below, provided courtesy of Polyproducts Corporation.

Epoxies: General Characteristics

1. Epoxy has very great adhesive strength.
2. Epoxy can be translucent, transparent, or opaque.
3. Cured (hard) epoxy can be handled very much like wood or metal.
4. Epoxy undergoes very little shrinkage (less than ½ percent) during the curing process.
5. Epoxy plastics are likely to chalk (get dull) or yellow if exposed to direct sunlight for long periods.
6. Epoxy can be cured with a wide range of hardeners, thus giving the user accurate control over the rate of the curing process.

7. Because epoxy is so powerful an adhesive, epoxy resins can be mixed with proportionally large quantities of fillers without being unreasonably weakened.

8. Epoxy resins are relatively expensive.

9. Toxicity: The principal hazard associated with epoxy resin systems is risk of dermatitis. Avoid all skin contact, especially with the hardener.

Polyesters: General Characteristics

1. Polyesters do not have great adhesive strength.

2. Polyesters can be opaque, translucent, or transparent to the point of being "water-clear."

3. Before hardening, polyester goes through a leatherlike stage, when it may be worked for special effects.

4. During the curing process, polyester shrinks up to 7 percent.

5. The appearance of polyester is affected less by sunlight than epoxy.

6. Polyesters may be used when the precise rate of cure is not critical.

7. Polyesters may be used with fiberglass or other reinforcing materials when transparency is not important.

8. Generally, polyester resin costs about half the price of epoxy.

9. Toxicity: The principal hazard associated with polyester resin is the styrene vapor given off by the resin. Good ventilation and the use of a cartridge mask are recommended. Also, the catalyst is a severe eye irritant, so protective glasses should be worn.

In light of the relative costs of the materials, it is a good rule of thumb to remember that epoxies should be used only when polyesters will not suffice.

Working with Polyester Resin

Resins are used for casting or coating. Pigment is added to the clear resin to change it to the desired color. Special pigments are available, such as pearlescence (pearl-like in appearance) and double-color pigment (which changes color in different light). Other additives, including metal powder (which creates the appearance of metal), ultraviolet-light stabilizer (used to retard yellowing or fading if the work is to be exposed to the sun for long periods), glitter, flexibilizer (to make the plastic flexible), glow in the dark, and internal mold release, may be combined with the resin. A catalyst, purchased with liquid resin, is used to harden it. (See *Sources of Supplies.*)

When working with plastics, the following precautions should be taken:
- Wear disposable plastic gloves or skin barrier cream.
- Wear a mask made specifically for protection against fumes and dust.
- Use good ventilation. For extended use, work outdoors or next to an exhaust fan.

Embedding Objects in Polyester Resin

Effects may be achieved with plastics that cannot be created with any other material. Embedment is a means of capturing and preserving objects by suspending them in a solid block of plastic. The plastic gives fragile objects strength and stops them from aging and decaying. Thus it is possible to incorporate otherwise unusable objects in a piece of jewelry.

Just about anything, including metal, plastic, shells, and photos can be embedded in plastic, so long as the object does not contain water. Even flowers and bugs can be embedded if they are dried first. The following is the method used by jeweler Bob Natalini to embed objects in polyester resin.

The Mold

The embedment may be made directly in a cavity carved or constructed in a piece of jewelry, in a mold constructed from sheets of glass, acetate sheet, oil-base clay, rubber, wax, sealed plaster, or any smooth material that is compatible with the resin. Plasticene (an oil-base nonhardening clay) or wax may be used to hold sheets of glass or acetate together to make the mold. A mold-release agent such as polyvinyl alcohol may be applied to the mold before pouring the resin to ensure easy removal of the casting.

A simple casting or embedment may be made in a plastic-coated-paper hot cup. After curing, the resulting plastic disc may be sawed with a jeweler's saw, filed, or machined to the desired shape.

Weighing and Mixing the Resin

Additives, pigment, and, in particular, the catalyst are added to the resin in specific proportions. Measuring by eye is risky and not recommended. A sensitive scale (a gram scale is best) will give controlled and easily duplicated results. Be certain to subtract the weight of the cup when doing your calculations. These ingredients are mixed with a wooden stirrer in a plastic-coated paper hot cup.

Begin by pouring the desired amount of resin into the cup. Add a small amount of resin thinner to facilitate the removal of bubbles. In addition, to avoid whipping bubbles into the resin, stir the ingredients slowly in a figure 8.

Next, measure and stir additives such as flexibilizer or metal powder into the resin. Never use more than 18 percent by weight of additives. Pigments (usually in paste form) are added until the desired color is achieved. Only a minimum amount of pigment is needed, for it is quite potent. When embedding objects, transparent pigments are used so that the object will remain visible.

A catalyst must be added to cure the plastic. Measurement of the catalyst must be precise. Too much catalyst will not allow time for bubbles to escape, and the excess heat created in quick curing may cause the work to shrink and crack. Too little catalyst will leave the resin tacky and not fully cured.

The thicker the casting, the lower the proportion of catalyst needed. The following is a list of suggested proportions of catalyst to resin. These ratios are calculated for working at a temperature of 70°F (21°C). Lower temperatures will slow down the curing process.

Thickness of Casting	Weight of Catalyst
2″ (5 cm)	⅛% (.00125)
1″ (2.5 cm)	¼% (.0025)
¾″ (2 cm)	½% (.005)
½″ (1.3 cm)	1% (.01)
¼″ (6 mm)	2% (.02)

Casting may be done in several layers. Castings that are thicker than 2″ (5 cm) should be executed in stages, allowing one layer to gel before adding another. Embedments are done in two layers of resin. When the object is set in place in the first layer, the top layer is poured to encapsulate the object. Do not let the first layer harden completely before pouring the next. The layers will blend together without evidence of their separate pourings.

Use less catalyst when adding a second layer to compensate for the heat being given off by the first layer. Curing will begin immediately after the catalyst is added and will be complete within twenty-four hours. A heat lamp may be used to speed the curing process. Keep the lamp at least 18″ (46 cm) away from the resin. Less time is needed for castings of ½″ (1.3 cm) or less. Surfaces exposed to air will remain slightly gummy and should be removed by filing and sanding.

After the plastic has cured and is removed from the mold, it may be sawed, filed, drilled, machined, and sanded with metal-working tools. Polish with a stitched muslin buff charged with stainless-steel polish.

Mold Variations

Try using burs of different shapes on a flexible shaft to cut depressions into a block of cast polyester resin. Fill the depressions with resin of a different color.

Try embedding objects that will protrude from the casting. Metal may be filed flush with the plastic to create a contrasting surface.

Lamination

The piece shown in figure 9–4 illustrates the technique of lamination. This lamination was made by pouring forty separate layers of colored resins.

Bob Natalini began by constructing the mold into which the layers were to be poured. The mold was made from sheets of glass, which were held together with wax. The melted wax was applied with a brush. The first layer of resin was made in the manner described above for embedding objects in polyester resin.

While waiting for the layer to gel, the second color resin was mixed. This process was repeated forty times until a thick, multicolor block was formed. The resin was allowed to cure for

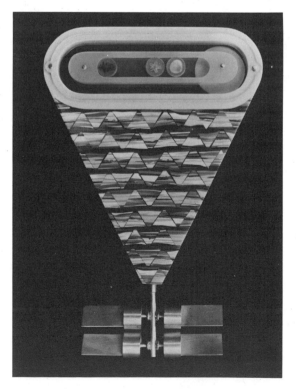

FIG. 9–4   Bob Natalini. Brooch of 18K gold, polyester, and natural objects that roll back and forth inside window tracks. 1974. *Courtesy of the artist.*

twenty-four hours after the last layer was poured, before it was removed from the mold.

In order to achieve such a triangular pattern, the multicolored block was sliced into thin sections with a jeweler's saw, and the sections were then cut into triangular tiles. To combine these tiles into a single unit, a second mold was constructed, this time in the shape of a large triangle. The small triangular tiles were layed into the mold and clear resin poured over them.

The piece was then sanded and polished. Additional elements, including the seashell, starfish, and irridescent beetle, were embedded separately. The different elements of the piece were held together primarily by riveting.

THE ARTIST SPEAKS: BOB NATALINI

My recent work takes the form of jewelry and sculpture. It is filled with diversity and contrasts and involves a great variety of materials. One reason for this is my interest in fusing activity, technology, the human, and the natural. Activity and technology are introduced through the use of functioning electronic circuitry to produce light and music sequences, sound, and movement. Some facets of the human element (satire, sexuality, humor, and pseudo-mysticism) are presented by using objects and materials discarded by society, photographs, and symbol-like drawings.

Having always been fond of nature, I am automatically drawn to include things such as bones, tropical beetles, and seashells in this scheme. Another very obvious aspect of my work is the importance of the surface, visual, and tactile qualities of many materials and contrasts developed among them in a piece. Some of the materials are wood, bone, colored silk, and plastics.

Working with Lexan

Lexan, a plastic that is made in rod, sheet, and other forms, is similar to, though stronger, than Plexiglas. It can be machined, cut, heat shaped, and hammer forged (though the latter is difficult), and it can be transparent, clear, or colored.

One jeweler who works with Lexan is Carey Smith, presently chairperson of the arts department at the Academy of the New Church, Bryn Athyn, Pennsylvania. In "Homage to the Queen" (figure 9–5), Smith used Lexan rods of various thicknesses and cut them to the desired lengths with a jeweler's saw. The rods were then shaped with coarse files and refined further with finer files and

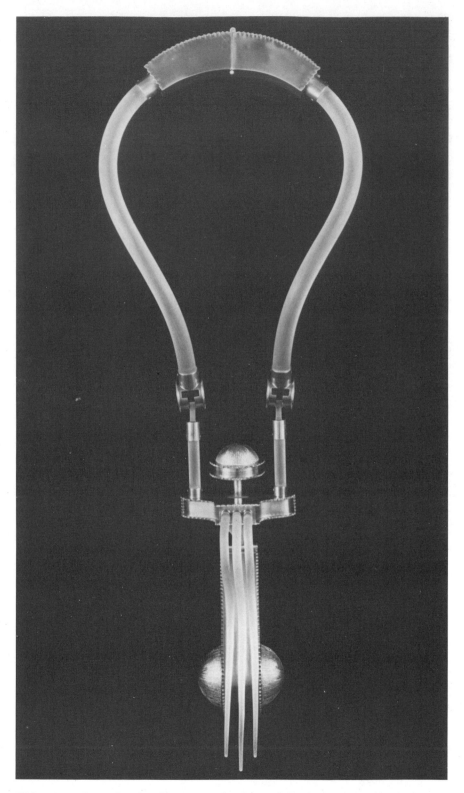

FIG. 9–5 Carey Smith. "Homage to the Queen." Neckpiece of sterling silver and Lexan. 1973. *Courtesy of the artist.*

varying grits of wet and dry emery paper. The fine emery finish was left without further polishing, leaving a matt finish.

After cutting, filing, and sanding, the pieces of Lexan were placed in a household oven set at approximately 320°F (160°C). The work was put on a tray and into the oven at about 250–275°F (121–135°C) and the heat increased slowly.

Heavy cotton gloves were worn when handling the hot plastic. In just a few minutes, the plastic became fairly soft and bendable, and it was quickly removed and shaped. Because the rods cool and stiffen quickly when removed from the heat, they must sometimes be shaped several times. It is helpful to have an assistant who can open the oven door, leaving your hands free.

Although this piece was not predried, the manufacturer recommends that it be if the Lexan is to remain clear. Otherwise, tiny bubbles appear, and it becomes milky white. This occurs because moisture is absorbed from the air, causing bubbles when heated. However, this effect may be used to advantage, if you choose.

To predry, heat the Lexan in an oven at a temperature of approximately 250°F (121 C). Drying time varies with the thickness of the sheet, but it takes a minimum of six hours.

After the Lexan is shaped, it can be polished further if a high shine is desired. The procedure is similar to that of polishing metal. Stainless-steel polish or other brand-name products made specifically for polishing plastics can be used. If you are polishing by machine, never allow heat to build up or the plastic may begin to melt. Heat is also minimized by avoiding pressing the work too hard against the buffing wheel. Move the work back and forth while polishing so that heat will not be concentrated in one spot. If the work does get hot, it can be left to cool before continuing, or immersed in cool water and dried.

Cutting, heat forming, and gluing acrylic are discussed in Chapter 10 in connection with creating displays. Those same techniques can be applied to jewelry making.

Tinting Plastic

Many plastics can be dyed in the same way that plastic eyeglasses are tinted, but the expensive equipment and dyes used by the optometric trade are unnecessary. Successful dying can be done with Rit liquid dyes and by following the directions on the bottle. Be careful not to boil the die while the plastic is immersed in it. (Plastic has a low melting point.)

For shading, immerse the plastic for longer periods to achieve a deeper tone. To remove unwanted color, use Rit's dye remover. Different plastics will take the dye differently, and the tint may fade over time.

Ceramic Jewelry

Because clay responds readily to pressure, it is a quick and simple medium for making jewelry. Clay jewelry can be primitive and rough or intricately sculpted and sophisticated.

Clay, as it comes from the earth, can be one of many colors, including white, yellow, red, brown, or black. Unless self-hardening or oven-hardening clay is used, a kiln is needed to fire the clay to its maturing temperature. Be certain that the kiln will fire to the maturing temperature of the specific clay that is used.

FIG. 9–6 Clay beads. Egyptian, New Kingdom. *The Metropolitan Museum of Art. Gift of Mrs. Edward S. Harkness, 1940.*

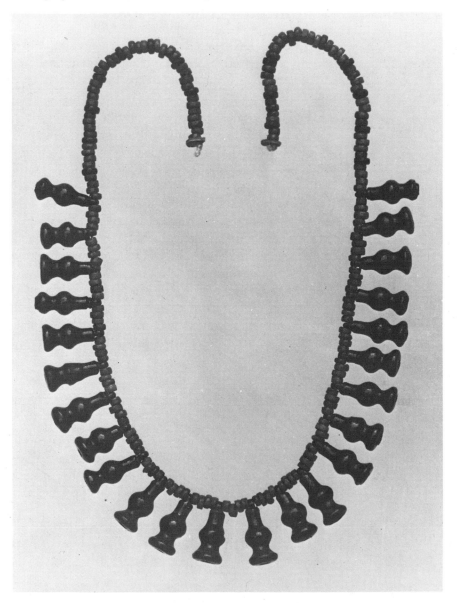

This temperature is usually written on the clay container or on literature from the manufacturer.

Many schools and private studios are willing to rent kiln space, and the cost should be minimal for small items such as jewelry. Small kilns can be purchased at a ceramic or enameling supply company. A kiln that can be regulated and its temperature increased slowly is suitable.

When working in clay, do not hesitate to combine different colors within a single piece of jewelry. Different colored clays can be combined to achieve a marbleized effect. Coloring agents such as cobalt oxide and copper oxide, available at a ceramic supply store, can be mixed into the clay.

Making Ceramic Beads

One of the major applications of clay in jewelry is making beads. Beads can be made in any shape and molded into recognizable forms, such as animals or figures, or into abstract forms. So long as the beads lie comfortably on the body, your imagination need not be constrained.

Beads are an ideal surface for creating textures. Kitchen utensils, files, sea shells, twigs, hair rollers, or just about anything found around the home and studio can be used. An inexpensive children's rubber printing set, purchased at a toy store, is ideal for printing words or creating textures by repeating and overlapping letters.

To make a bead, roll out the clay into a ball or coil. To create more than one bead from a coil of clay, use a wire or thin knife to slice the coil into sections. Width, length, shape, and size, as well as texture, can be varied to create an interesting necklace. The hole is then made with a piece of metal tubing or wire of the appropriate diameter. A piece of coat-hanger wire will work well, and it can be rolled within the hole to enlarge it. Remember that clay will shrink when fired, so make the hole and bead larger to allow for shrinkage. The percentage of shrinkage varies with each clay.

Textures can be applied before or after the hole is made, or, while the bead is on the wire, it can be easily rolled over the textured surface.

Small pieces of clay can be added to the bead or pendant by scratching the surfaces to be joined with a sharp tool and applying clay "glue," known as *slip,* between the surfaces. Slip is made from clay dissolved in water to the consistency of yogurt.

Making Other Clay Shapes

To make a sheet of clay, or a slab, use a rolling pin, dowel, or other cylindrical object to roll the clay to the desired thickness. Plastic wrap can be placed between the clay and the roller to prevent sticking and to keep the roller clean. The slab should be $^1/_{16}$″ (2 mm) or thinner. Use a thin knife or pin tool to cut out your shape. A paper pattern may be used to cut out a number of identical shapes. Any number of holes can be poked into this shape depending on how the beads will be strung.

After the clay has been fired once in a kiln, it can be glazed, painted, or stained. Acrylic paint is fine for coloring the fired clay, and it may be used as a stain when thinned with water to a consistency where the color will soak into the clay.

When glazes are used, the beads must be fired a second time in order to melt the glaze. This creates a glasslike finish on the clay. The firing temperatures of glazes vary, and the capabilities of your kiln may affect your choice of glaze. Glazed beads are fired on a bead rack, consisting of two kiln supports across which lengths of Nichrome wire are spanned. Its function is to prevent glazed beads from touching and fusing with any surface or with each other. Be certain that the hole through which the wire is strung is free from glaze.

Apply the glaze to the entire piece or to specific areas, using a small brush. Different glazes can be combined on a single bead. If detail is desired, use underglazes, which impart color and do not run or drip during firing. Underglazed designs are covered with a coat of clear glaze for permanence.

Completed beads can be strung on a leather thong, fishing line, shoelace, ribbon, or chain and combined with seeds, shells, metallic beads and washers, wood, sequins, or other beads. When combining materials, consider the weight of the finished piece. Light materials such as sequins will compensate for the heaviness of large clay beads, as in the stoneware, porcelain, and sequin necklace by Judy Moonelis shown in the color section.

Wood Inlays

Woods exist in nature in a variety of colors—from white to yellow, orange, red, brown, and black. Their grain patterns vary in size as well as in shape. Unusual growths within the wood, such as burls and knots, create even greater variety and can be used creatively by the jeweler.

Hardwoods are preferred over softwoods by most jewelers. Hardwood trees can be distinguished from softwood trees by their broad leaves rather than cones and needles. The advantages of hardwoods for use in jewelry are primarily their varied colors, close-grained patterns, and greater strength.

Walnut, ebony, mahogany, cocobolo, zebra, rosewood, and oak

are a few of the hardwoods. Although some may be native to your area, others may be purchased at lumberyards or through supply houses that deal in unusual woods. Scraps from a cabinetmaker and pieces of old wooden objects and furniture are also a good source for the jeweler. Some jewelry supply houses such as Allcraft offer a selection of hardwoods sold in small quantity. Woods are also available in thin sheets, or veneers.

Wood may be laminated, inlayed into wood or metal of a contrasting color, or used as a base into which metal is inlayed. In addition, it may be sculpted, using files and a flexible shaft fitted with various burs, ground and mixed with epoxy for inlaying, or set in metal and treated as a gem. Wood is often held in place with a bezel, glue, or rivets. All soldering and finishing of the metal must be completed before adding the wood.

Epoxy-Wood Inlay

A wood-epoxy inlay looks like a slab of wood, but it is much easier to use. The painstaking job of cutting and filing the wood to the exact size of the cavity in the metal is avoided. Instead, the wood fills the entire area, leaving no gaps. It is quick and simple, and a number of small scraps of wood may be ground to fill a large area.

Inlaying is done after the piece has been otherwise completed. The work seen in figure 9–8 (the belt buckle in Chapter 2) was constructed by sweat soldering a pierced sheet of metal onto a background sheet. Ebony and epoxy were used to inlay the piece after it was soldered, sanded, and polished.

The ebony-epoxy inlay is made by grinding the ebony with a coarse file (figure 9–7) or a rough bur in a flexible shaft. (See page 31 for an explanation of the flexible shaft.) Then epoxy and ebony filings are mixed in a ratio of approximately one-quarter epoxy to three-quarters ebony. The mixture should be thick. Use long drying (two-hour) epoxy to allow time for working. The more ebony that is used in proportion to the epoxy, the darker the wood will look when it sets. Be certain to record the ratio used in the event that any patching is necessary. This will ensure that the color can be matched.

When the mixture is well combined, spread it into the cells of the piece with a toothpick, making sure to fill all areas over the level of the metal (figure 9–8). Allow it to set completely (overnight). For setting time, see the instructions on the epoxy packaging.

When the inlay is completely set, file with a coarse file, making sure not to touch the metal (figure 9–9). Use masking tape to protect the metal from scraches. After filing off most of the excess mixture, sand and polish with successively finer grits of wet and dry emery paper (figure 9–10). Begin with 180 grit and work down to

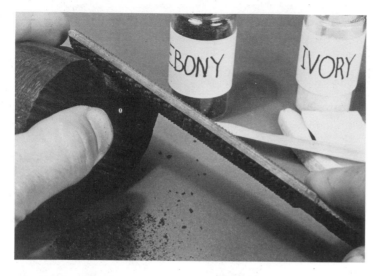

FIG. 9–7   File the ebony to make ebony dust.

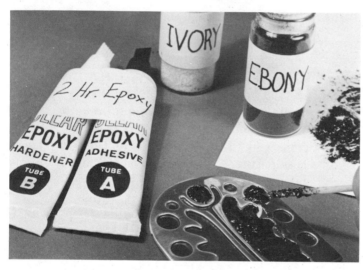

FIG. 9–8   Mix the ebony with two-hour epoxy and use a toothpick to inlay the mixture.

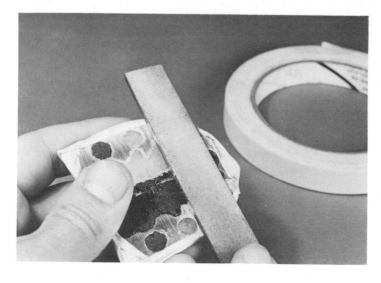

FIG. 9–9   Protect the metal with masking tape while filing the rough surface flat.

FIG. 9–10   Refine the surface further with emery paper.

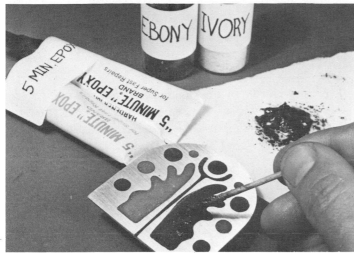

FIG. 9–11   Fill pits with a mxiture of ebony and five-minute epoxy.

600 grit. Wood can be polished further with tripoli applied to a buff.

Fill any pits in the inlay with a freshly mixed batch of epoxy and ebony (figure 9–11). Use five-minute epoxy for this touch-up work. Resand any filled pits, polish, and wash with mild soap and water. A few drops of oil rubbed into the finished wood will preserve it and give a slight shine.

Epoxy Inlay Variations

The inlay procedure can be done with any materials that can be crushed or ground, such as abalone shell. To crush the shell, place it between sheets of newspaper or in a cloth to prevent it from scattering and hit it with a mallet. It can be broken down further in a mortar and pestle. Mix the crushed shell with epoxy and spread it into the cavity. Finally, finish by filing with a fine file. With abalone, no further finishing is necessary.

Ivory can be ground and inlayed in the same manner as ebony. It is polished with white rouge on a stitched cotton buff.

Other materials that can be inlayed with epoxy are mixed metals, all woods, crushed turquoise, alabaster or any soft stone, crushed coral, and dry color pigments and powdered enamels. (See figure 9–12 for an interesting combination.) Experiment with different mixtures to find out which works best for your purposes.

THE ARTIST SPEAKS: DONNA MATLES

I tend toward the direct techniques of construction and try to reveal the inherent qualities of the stones, woods, or shell as they interact with each other and metal. It is the overall visual impact that interests me more than technical acrobatics.

THE ARTIST SPEAKS: JEAN BATTLES-IRVIN

I work in mixed media, mostly in fiber techniques and drawing. The fiber techniques are the traditional ones—macramé, crochet, tatting, wrapping, stuffing, weaving—but it is the combining of the various techniques and the materials that I find new and exciting, and which produces a certain magic. I love the idea of something that can be

FIG. 9–12 Joyce Kaplan. Pendant of sterling silver, turquoise, inlayed ebony, and abalone shell. *Courtesy of the artist.*

FIG. 9–13 Donna Matles. Buckle of vermillion, ebony, paulhera, brass, and bone. *Courtesy of the artist. Photo by David Halpern.*

worn (functional) and also exists as an art object (aesthetic). The line between "craft" and "fine art" becomes very fuzzy for me.

Although I like metals and precious and semiprecious stones, it is exciting to me to be able to make art with ordinary materials.

Weaving with Metal

Virtually any textile process—coiling, braiding, knitting, macramé, weaving—is adaptable to metal. Techniques must be modified to take into account the metal's unique qualities, however. Weaving with metal has some advantages over using yarn: In addition to holding its shape easily, metal can be polished, textured, and subjected to all of the techniques, such as soldering, used in making jewelry.

Choose an appropriate form, size, and type of metal for each weaving project. The degree of flexibility of the metal is most important. Different metals and their alloys possess different degrees of flexibility. The most flexible and popular metals for weaving are copper, fine silver, and 18K gold. However, other metals usually can be used successfully. To increase flexibility, anneal the metals before working in textile techniques.

The gauge of the metal must also be taken into consideration. Thinner metal is easy to manipulate, and wire can be drawn as thin as thread. Sheet metal is also available in a variety of gauges. It can be drawn thin enough for easy cutting into strips with shears. Aluminum foil is an example of just how thin and flexible sheet metal can be.

Wire can be purchased in coated form for variety in color and protection against oxidation. The piece by Mary Lee Hu, shown in

FIG. 9–14   Gammy Miller. Necklace of waxed linen and clam-shell fragment. Half-hitched. *Courtesy of the artist. Photo by Ken Kimerling.*

figure 9–15 was made with lacquer-coated copper wire. Colored wire can be found in old motors or purchased in an electronics supply store.

THE ARTIST SPEAKS: GAMMY MILLER

I am basically self-taught and come to knotting circuitously. But for the last six years, it has been an answer to a lifetime of collecting things too many to keep. I like being around bits and pieces of shells and bones, particularly those marked by time and weather. As a jeweler sets precious stones in precious metals, I set small common things, fragments, into fiber to make of them a precious whole.

How to Weave

Weaving involves the interlacing of the weft (horizontal strands) with the warp (vertical strands). The warp is strung first and the weft is woven into it. The warp consists of an uneven number of strands. It may be continuous and strung through drilled holes, wrapped around soldered pegs, or made up of individual strands attached to the main portion of the piece by solder or rivets. Another approach is to tie the warp to a frame.

FIG. 9–15   Mary Lee Hu. Choker of fine and sterling silver, 24K gold, and lacquered copper. 1978. *Courtesy of the artist.*

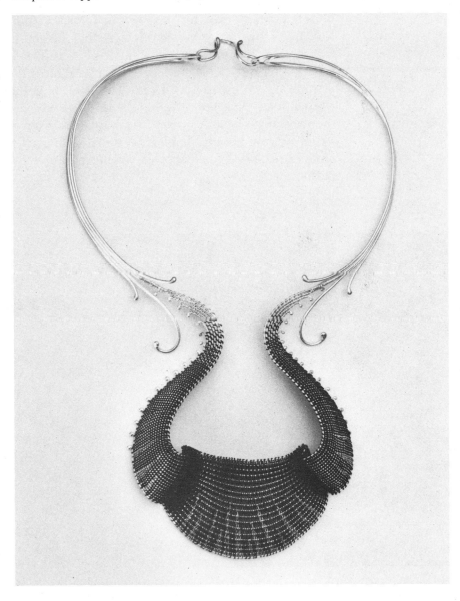

The weft is passed over and under the warp strands. Strands grouped at regular intervals create patterns. For a plain weave, the weft is woven in a pattern of under one, over one.

A simple variation on this stitch is done by passing the weft under two strands and then over two strands. The use of different metals to create color contrast will accentuate a pattern. Vertical stripes can be made by alternating the color of metal used in each row so that the raised strands over a particular warp strand are always the same color.

Weaving on a Loom

Metal weaving may be done on a loom in the same manner as working with yarn. One jeweler, Arline Fisch, is an innovator in this area and the author of a book on textile techniques in metal (see *Bibliography*). Her piece shown in figure 9–16 is an example of weaving with wire on a loom. The loom is helpful in keeping the warp strands taut, and it increases the ability to control the shape of the weaving. Looms range in complexity from the simple frame loom, which merely holds the warp straight, to more complex models, which are capable of raising strands of warp for intricate patterning.

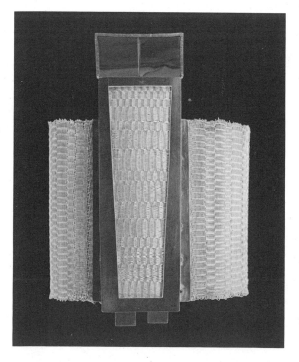

FIG. 9–16   Arline Fisch. "Land Forms." Bracelet/brooch. Bracelet band: fine silver, loom woven. Clasp becomes a brooch when detached. Clasp: sterling silver and picture jasper, loom-woven silver insert. 1977. *Courtesy of the artist*.

Using Woven Forms

A woven area may be created directly on a work in progress, or a completed weaving may be added to a piece. The warp may be strung directly on the piece by drilling small holes into the metal to accept the warp. To attach a completed weaving, a frame may be riveted around the woven material, concealing the loose ends and trapping it in place. It may also be sewn on with a separate piece of wire. Soldering is not advisable when the metal used in the weaving is thin.

Coiling

Coiling is one of the techniques used in basketry that is readily adapted to jewelry making. In addition, the rafia, grass, or yarn usually used in coiling baskets can be adapted too. Coiling is a simple process, easily mastered, providing great possibilities for form, texture, color and pattern. Coiling may also be combined with other processes, as has been done in figure 9–17 and 9–18.

By using this technique, it is simple to make a piece of jewelry with only a few tools. You will need two pairs of smooth-jawed pliers, a wire cutter, a pointed tool such as a scribe, and two gauges of round wire. Use the thicker wire for the core and the thinner one for the weft, which will be wound around the core. If you are limited to a single gauge of wire, a few strands can be twisted together to make a thicker core.

Wire for Coiling

In coiling, the core must be strong enough to support the coiling and, at the same time, maleable enough to bend so that curved forms can be made. Approximately 18- or 16-gauge wire is good for the core. The weft must be very flexible in order to withstand continual tight bending around the core. Wire for the weft can be 22- or 24-gauge or thinner.

Gold, copper, fine silver, sterling silver, and brass are all fine for this purpose. Fine silver, gold, and copper are the more maleable and can therefore be used in thicker gauges. Different metals and gauges can be combined in a single piece to add variety in color and thickness. Coiling can be small and delicate or large and bold depending on the gauge used. Experiment with a variety of gauges and metals to see which are most suitable.

The amount of wire needed will depend on your design. A great deal more weft is needed than core. You may wish to solder the ends of the core and the weft together before you begin coiling.

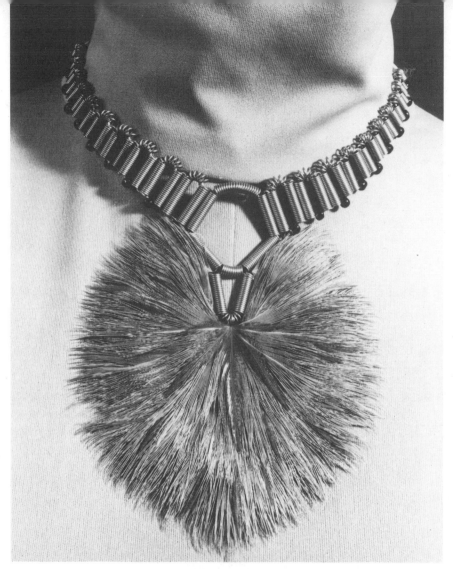

FIG. 9–17 Jennison.
Neckpiece of gold-filled wire
(coiled) with ring-necked
pheasant, golden pheasant, and
banty-rooster feathers glued to a
leather backing. *Photo by R. A.
Lafande.*

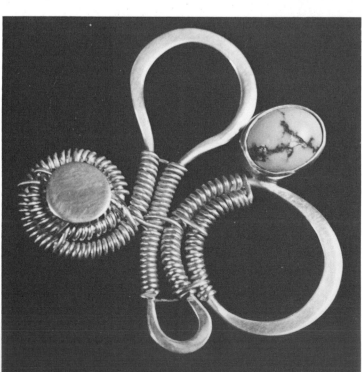

FIG. 9–18 Coiled pin of
sterling silver, 14K gold, and
turquoise.

How to Coil

Begin by wrapping the weft around the core for approximately ⅜″ (9 mm) in tight, even coils (figure 9–19). Spiral the wire and take a connecting stitch with the weft after every few coils (figure 9–20). The wire will act as its own needle when a stitch must be taken in a tight spot. Use a pointed instrument such as a scribe or compass point to help spread the wires where it is difficult to stitch. The more securing stitches that are taken, the stronger the piece will be. Continue coiling and securing as you go until you have made a form of the desired size.

Using this coiling technique, almost any shape can be made. To make a vessel form, wind the coil in an upward spiral as you work. Lay the core on the inside edge of the previous row when you want the form to get narrower (figure 9–21), and on the outside when you want it to get wider.

When you need to lengthen the core, just add a new piece of wire. Use a file to taper approximately ⅜″ (9 mm) of the two ends of the wires being joined. Join them by overlapping the tapered ends and coiling tightly over both wires. These core wires may be held more securely by soldering before coiling. Because the two ends have been tapered, there will be no additional thickness, and the joint will not be visible when covered by the weft.

Coiling Variations

The material from which either the core or the weft is made can be changed in order to add variety to a piece. The weft can be wrapped around a core of natural material, such as a shell or twig (figure 9–22) or threaded through a bead, metal washer, or a hole in sheet metal. Lovely coiled jewelry can be fashioned from yarn, embroidery thread, or any materials that are both strong and flexible. Also, materials such as threads and wires can often be combined.

Braiding and Twisting

Three or more wires or thin strips of sheet metal may be braided together. The wire should be flexible so that you can easily bend it with your hands. Different metals may be used to create colored patterns.

To braid, hold the wires at one end in a bench vise. Space wires evenly, one next to the other. Of course, the more wires used, the wider the band will be. The first strand on the right (the weft) is always woven through the other strands (the warp). The right hand is used to braid the weft over and under the warp. Begin braiding

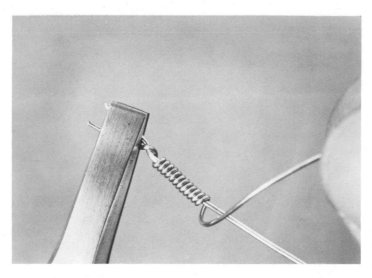

FIG. 9–19 Begin coiling by wrapping the weft around the core. Pliers may be used to hold the ends.

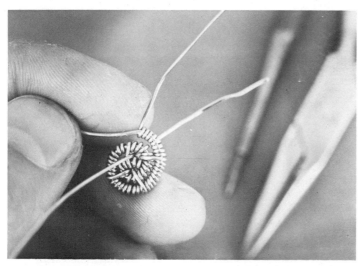

FIG. 9–20 Take a connecting stitch at intervals in order to connect adjoining wires.

FIG. 9–21 To make a concave form, stitch the coiled wire onto the inner edge of the previous row.

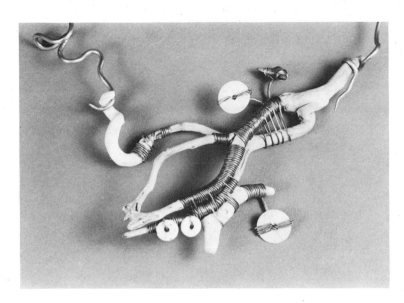

FIG. 9–22   Coiled necklace of driftwood, shell, wormcase, brass, sterling silver, shark's tooth, and coral.

FIG. 9–23   David Poston. Necklace of whipped cotton on hemp with silver. *Photo by the artist.*

FIG. 9–24   Braided wires.

over and under the wires, including the last one. At the end of the first row, this weft (now the last wire) becomes part of the warp, and a new weft (the new first wire) is woven through the warp (figure 9–24). Repeat until you have achieved the desired size. Note that the weft always begins by going *over* the first wire of the warp.

Braided wire can be incorporated in a larger piece or used on its own as a bracelet, for example, with the ends of the wires balled.

Different shapes, colors, and thicknesses of wire may be twisted together in any combination. A square, rectangular, half-round, or triangular wire may be twisted as a single strand, or two or more wires may be twisted together. Round wire must be twisted with at least one other wire in order for the twist to be visible. The wires being twisted together should be of equal strength.

Before twisting, anneal the wire. Hold the wires at one end in a bench vise and at the other end in either a hand vise or a hand drill. Use a hand drill for twisting thin wire (figure 9–25). To hold the wire in the drill, tighten a hook in the chuck and loop the wire around it. Twist the wires by turning the drill or hand vise. Maintain tension on the wires while twisting in order to create an even, straight twist.

There are many variations on the basic twist. Wires may be twisted together and then twisted a second time with other twisted or straight wires. They may be twisted in different directions and then combined. For contrast, sections of a single strand of wire may be twisted and other sections left straight. This is accomplished by placing smooth-jawed pliers or a vise grip at the point where you want to begin the twist. The pliers will keep the wire behind it from twisting. Use a piece of leather to protect the metal from being marred by the pliers.

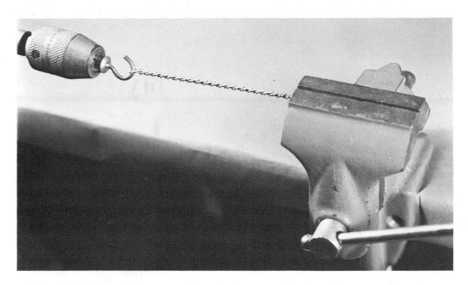

FIG. 9–25   Use a drill to twist thin wire.

Twisted wire may also be run through a rolling mill or flattened with a hammer. Be careful when flattening wires at their intersections; if they become too thin, they may break.

When soldering the two ends of the twisted wire together to form a loop or a bangle bracelet, cut the ends at the point in the twist that will allow the pattern to remain unbroken after soldering. If soldering is done properly, there will be no evidence of a soldered joint.

Jewelry Displays

10

The way jewelry is displayed can significantly influence the way it is appreciated and enjoyed. A good display will provide a pleasant atmosphere and capture viewers' attention, inviting them to examine the work in detail. Poorly displayed work, on the other hand, is often overlooked and therefore never given a chance to speak for itself. The overall effect should be one in which the display does not overpower or distract attention from the work but rather provides the best context for viewing.

Props

Although props are necessary to support the work, they should never clutter or distract. The eye should be carried smoothly from one piece to the other, allowing enough space for each piece to be seen on its own. If space is limited, it is often better to display fewer pieces rather than crowd the work.

To unify the display, it is advisable to choose props that follow a theme. Repetition of subject, color, shape, and material promotes unity. The display props may be spray painted a single color for simplicity. White or black is often the most effective.

Some jewelers construct a display unit as an integral part of their jewelry (figures 10–1 and 10–2). In this way, the jewelry functions as a small sculpture or wall hanging.

A number of jewelry display firms sell pads, busts, ring holders, and other items specifically designed for displaying jewelry. These are the type often seen in jewelry store windows. They are available in many materials, shapes, and colors. (See *Sources of Supplies*.)

FIG. 10–1 Bruce Metcalf. "Man in the City" and "A Light Lost at Sea." Pins displayed on stands. Silver, acrylic, brass, enamel, pen, and ink. 1978. *Courtesy of the artist.*

FIG. 10–2 Gene and Hiroko Pijanowski. "Wall Hanging with Detachable Pendant/Brooch." Plexiglas, brass, copper, silver, silk, and Shakudo (Japanese alloy). Carved, inlayed, and constructed. *Courtesy of the artists.*

Ordinary objects are sometimes even more effective than the elaborate, expensive displays sold commercially. The following are some of the possible props and materials used for jewelry display. They must all be used sparingly and tastefully in order not to detract from the jewelry.

Food. Bread sticks, bagels, rolls coated with plastic resin for preservation; vegetables; eggs; marshmallows.

Construction materials. Bricks; metal, plastic, or ceramic pipes; wooden dowels; wooden beams; spools.

Natural objects. Shells, rocks, driftwood, moss.

Art and craft materials. Balls of yarn, jeweler's tools, spools of thread.

Toys. Wooden blocks; dolls; building toys such as Legos, Lincoln Logs, and Tinkertoys; multiples of a small toy such as toy cars, sprayed a single color.

Household objects. Flower pots, garden tools, egg cartons, antiques, clothing (figure 10–3).

Soft sculpture. Simple forms such as a snake shape can be sewn and stuffed.

FIG. 10–3   Display by Joy Hand.

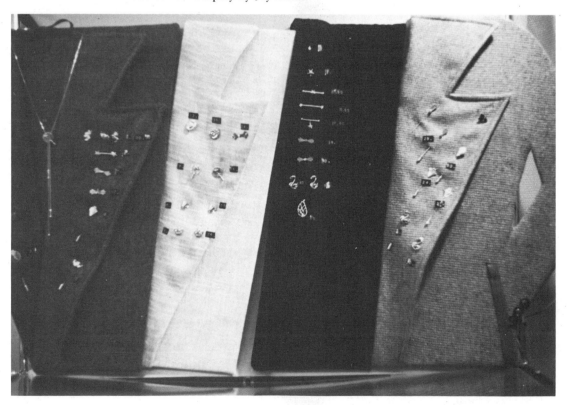

Styrofoam. Styrofoam shapes such as cones, spheres, and rectangles may be purchased. Jersey can be stretched over the shapes, which have been cut to size with an ordinary household knife. Spheres can be sliced in half so that they will lie flat. Using T pins, the fabric ends may be pinned in place on the underside of the styrofoam form.

Fabric. A background may be chosen for texture, contrast, and color, using fabrics such as velvet, suede cloth, and felt, which absorb light and do not have distracting, large textures. They can be stretched over cardboard shapes to create individual backgrounds for one or a grouping of jewelry pieces.

Display-case background materials. The following are some suggestions for background materials: fine sand, coffee beans, popcorn, nuts, stones, lentils, marshmallows, cork, slate, tiles, mirrors, noodles, and wood chips. Wooden, metal, or acrylic boxes may be constructed to hold the background material in one large display area or in a number of separate compartments.

Plaster-cast props. A mold for casting a prop can be made of plasticene. Figure 10–4 shows a finger mold made using this technique. The mold was made in a cardboard box about 4″ (10 cm) deep. (Try a paper milk container.) Fill the box with plasticene (an oil-base clay that does not harden) to within 1″ (2.5 cm) of the top. Then stick your fingers into the plasticene and remove them gently. (Or use an object which can be removed without destroying the shape of the mold.) Now mix the plaster. Always add dry plaster to the water until the plaster no longer sinks and makes a mound on the top of the water. Then mix the plaster thoroughly and pour it into the mold. Fill the box to the top. You will have to work quickly in order to finish pouring before the plaster begins to set. After a few hours, the plaster can be removed from the plasticine. You may like the color imparted by the plasticene residue, or you may wash the cast in cold water until it is a sparkling white.

Acrylic Display Props

Acrylic comes in different forms such as rods, domes, cubes, sheets, and tubes and may be sawed, drilled, heat formed, and glued to create excellent props. Its light weight, strength, workability, and transparency contribute to its popular use in making displays.

Acrylic can be used in combination with other materials, such as wood. Wood beams may be cut to varied heights and capped with an acrylic dome. Holes are drilled in the flange of the dome and screws or wires inserted to hold the dome securely on the wood.

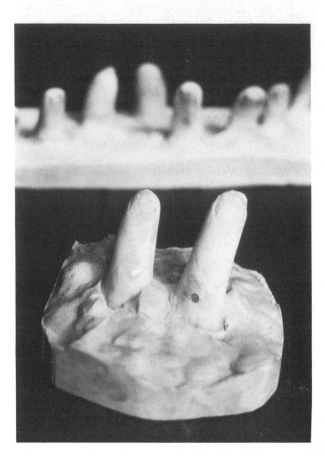

FIG. 10–4 Display prop cast with plaster in a plasticine mold.

Cutting Acrylic

Acrylic is cut with a saw or by scribing and breaking. In either case, the protective backing should be left on when cutting.

To cut acrylic by scribing and breaking, the sheet should be ¼″ (6 mm) thick or less. Although other knives can be used, it is preferable to use a scribe made specifically for this purpose. Using a straightedge as a guide, scribe the line to be cut seven to ten times, until it is cut well into the surface (figure 10–5). Then place the sheet with the scribed line facing upward over a dowel or broomstick (figure 10–6). To break the acrylic, apply pressure on the short side of the cut, while holding the other side firmly down. For small pieces, use pliers to break along the scribed line.

In order to cut curved lines, use a jeweler's, coping, band, or jig saw. Use a fine-tooth blade on the jig saw.

To achieve a polished surface on the cut edges, first file and then remove the file marks using a sharp piece of metal, such as the back of a hacksaw blade (figure 10–7). The surface can be sanded and polished with a fine white abrasive such as stainless steel polish or white diamond on a muslin buff (figure 10–8). A second polishing with an uncharged buff will complete the process.

FIG. 10–5 Score the Plexiglas with a scorer held against a metal ruler. *Courtesy of Rohm and Haas Co.*

FIG. 10–6 Break the Plexiglas over a dowel with the scribed surface facing up. *Courtesy of Rohm and Haas Co.*

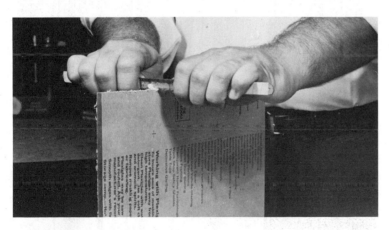

FIG. 10–7 Smooth the edge of the Plexiglas with an old hacksaw blade. *Courtesy of Rohm and Haas Co.*

FIG. 10–8 Polish the edges with a fine white abrasive on a muslin buff. *Courtesy of Rohm and Haas Co.*

Cementing Acrylic

Acrylic can be made to adhere to itself by using a special solvent available expressly for this purpose. The protective backing should be removed before cementing. Edges to be cemented should be sanded to a satin finish but not polished. The pieces to be attached are held together with masking tape where feasible. The cement is applied with a small brush, or preferably a syringe applicator (figure 10–9). The solvent will flow along the seam by capillary action, and the surfaces will bind after being held together for a few minutes.

Heat Forming Acrylic

After acrylic has been cut, it can be shaped by heat forming. To heat-form sheet acrylic along a straight line, use a strip heater. Strip heaters can be purchased at a plastics supply house, or you can make your own, as described below.

The acrylic is placed across the strip heater along the line where the bend is desired (figure 10–10). The heater will heat the line locally to 290°F (143°C) to 325°F (163°C). At this temperature, the plastic can be easily bent by hand. Bend with the heated side on the outside of the bend. Bending the sheet before it is soft will cause small internal fractures to appear. Hold the acrylic in position until it cools for a few minutes. After cooling, it will hold its shape indefinitely.

Making a Strip Heater

This acrylic strip heater is made using a Briskeat RH-36 heating element, manufactured by Brisco Manufacturing Company, Columbus, Ohio. The instructions come courtesy of Rohm and Haas

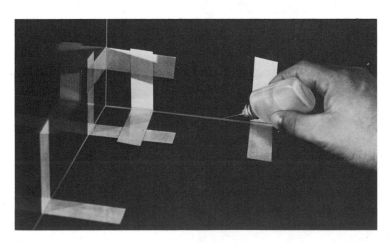

FIG. 10–9 Use masking tape to hold the Plexiglas sheets together while applying the solvent.

FIG. 10–10 To heat form along a straight line, place the acrylic across the strip heater along the line where the bend is desired. *Courtesy of Rohm and Haas Co.*

Company. The instructions call for asbestos paper, which can be hazardous. Unfortunately there is no suggested substitute.

1. Cut a piece of ½" (1.3 cm) plywood 6" × 42" (15 × 106.7 cm).

2. Cut two ¼" (6 mm) plywood strips 2⅝" × 36" (6.7 × 91.5 cm).

3. Center the two strips (2) on top of the base (1), leaving a ¾" (2 cm) channel down the center and nail to base.

4. Cut two pieces of heavy-duty aluminum foil 6" × 36" (15 × 91.5 cm) and fold to fit in the ¾" (2 cm) channel.

5. Attach a ground wire to the aluminum foil with a nail, as shown in figure 10–11. The ground wire should be long enough to attach to a common ground, such as the cover-plate screw on an electrical outlet.

6. Cut two pieces of asbestos paper 6¼" × 36" (16 × 91.5 cm) and fold to fit the ¾" (2 cm) channel on top of the aluminum foil. Staple asbestos paper and aluminum foil to ¼" (6 mm) plywood strips (2) along the outside edges.

7. Lay the Briskeat RH-36 heating element in the channel. Drive a nail 1½" (3.8 cm) from each end of the base (1) along a center line and tie the end strings of the heating element to the nails.

8. Slide the two pieces of the plug together. Attach the ground wire to a common ground and plug the strip heater into a 110-volt outlet.

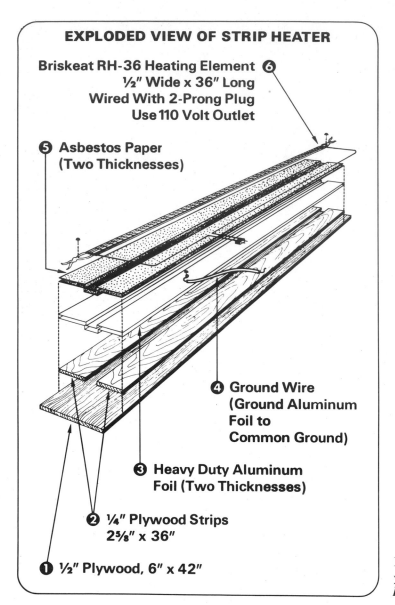

EXPLODED VIEW OF STRIP HEATER

Briskeat RH-36 Heating Element ➏
½" Wide x 36" Long
Wired With 2-Prong Plug
Use 110 Volt Outlet

➎ Asbestos Paper
(Two Thicknesses)

➍ Ground Wire
(Ground Aluminum
Foil to
Common Ground)

➌ Heavy Duty Aluminum
Foil (Two Thicknesses)

➋ ¼" Plywood Strips
2⅝" x 36"

➊ ½" Plywood, 6" x 42"

FIG. 10–11 Assembling your strip heater. *Courtesy of Rohm and Haas Co.*

Display Cases

Display cases may be made in any shape from virtually any material. They may be placed vertically or horizontally, braced on a wall or on a stand. Displays should be portable and easy to assemble and dismantle, as well as steady, durable, and attractive.

Display structures may be purchased ready-made, or they may be custom-made by a professional carpenter or by the jeweler. One company, Abstracta, makes a modular system of tubes and connectors that is adaptable to most display needs (figure 10–12). Shelves and walls can be made from acrylic sheet, glass, Masonite, or any rigid material. (See *Sources of Supplies*.)

FIG. 10–12   Kathryn Downs's display using the Abstracta System.

Display cases may be constructed from such traditional materials as wood (barn, plywood, Masonite, hardwood), acrylic sheet, glass, or from more unusual materials such as ladders, barrels, bins, boxes, and crates.

Lighting

Lighting may be used to dramatically highlight individual pieces or to illuminate a broad area. Lights may be built directly into a display case or attached to walls, cases, screens, or poles. If built into a case, provide ventilation holes so that heat can escape. Clamp-on lights are excellent for situations where portability is required. The type of clamp-on lights used by photographers are not suitable for use over extended periods, so purchase lights that have slotted shades to allow heat to escape. Lights should always be aimed in a direction that will not interfere with the viewer's vision. A visit to galleries, craft fairs, and jewelry stores will show a variety of lighting situations that can be adapted to your own needs.

Signs

Providing information such as titles, dates, materials used, and more general information about the jeweler's background and techniques is another aspect to be considered in displays. Signs can be made by a professional or by the exhibitor. The following are a few methods that are often used.

Calligraphic lettering. Calligraphy can be done with an inexpensive lettering pen, a variety of pen points for different types of lettering, and inks of different colors. For script lettering, a special script-point pen is available. Chisel-tip markers can also be used; they come in different sizes for small or large lettering.

Transfer alphabets. These letters, available in art supply stores, will adhere to a smooth surface when rubbed with a dull-pointed pencil.

Typing. IBM typewriters, among others, have changeable elements that permit the use of different size and styles of lettering. Colored ribbons are also available.

Lettering machines for embossing. These are inexpensive machines that are operated by hand and are available at a stationery store. Individual letters are pressed into a colored tape when the handles of the machine are squeezed together. The tape will adhere to most surfaces when the protective backing is removed.

Professional signs. By looking in the Yellow Pages, under "Signs," you can find wooden, plastic, handpainted, neon, metal, engraved, silkscreened, or just about any imaginable type of sign made professionally.

Photographs. Photography is another way to present information and enhance a display. Large, blown-up photos of the jeweler at work or of individual pieces of jewelry are an effective means of drawing attention to a display.

Security

Measures should be taken to help prevent theft of jewelry on display. Work may be exhibited in a showcase with entry accessible only to the exhibitor, or if left open to be handled by the viewer, it could be attached to the display fixtures in various ways. Consider using a U pin or thin elastic string. The pin is easily removed when trying on the piece. The elastic acts as a tether, allowing the work to be handled while it remains attached to the display. All means of securing the work should be as inconspicuous as possible.

To keep track of your work, it is advisable to show only one piece at a time and help only one customer at a time. This minimizes confusion. A fabric pad designed specifically for showing jewelry will help to limit and control the area in which the piece is viewed. Another means of keeping track of the number of pieces taken from the display at one time is to temporarily mark any vacant space with a paper dot so that a missing piece can be easily spotted.

Layout

The general layout of a display booth should take into account the number of people expected as well as the traffic flow. A display that is cramped and difficult to enter will discourage viewers. Instead, viewers should be led from one case to another easily and without confusion as to what has or has not been seen. You may also want to consider the addition of seating for yourself and customers.

Health Hazards

11

There is a growing awareness of the health hazards presented by exposure to poisonous substances in our environment. The jeweler is exposed to an extensive variety of materials used in such processes as soldering, etching, casting, and polishing. The hazards of working with most of these substances can be greatly diminished, and perhaps removed entirely, if the proper precautions are taken. Therefore, the jeweler must know the risks involved in working with such substances and the appropriate remedies.

Substances enter the body through the skin, the digestive system, and inhalation. Many are not harmful and are safely used or eliminated by normal bodily functions, while some create only minor discomfort, which clears up shortly after exposure. However, some commonly used substances are toxic, and their effects are particularly insidious because they are not felt until the condition has progressed beyond the point of reversal. Though a short period of exposure to some of these substances may not be harmful, the cumulative effects can be dangerous.

Safety Precautions

Many precautions can be taken to deal with various health and safety hazards.

Substitutions

Some materials such as asbestos and benzene are highly toxic and should be avoided if at all possible. They may be replaced by less hazardous materials with equivalent functions. For example, soft asbestos may be replaced by kiln brick. Substitutes for specific materials are discussed later in this chapter.

Respirators

Wear a respirator to prevent breathing dust, fumes, and mists. Specific filters and cartridges are designed for specific contaminants and should be used only as recommended. Cartridges will protect against inhaling acid-gas and dust and metal fumes. For working with solvents and resins, an organic vapor cartridge is used. Filters and cartridges must be changed regularly to ensure effectiveness. Only those respirators approved and labeled by NIOSH (National Institute of Occupational Safety and Health) should be used.

Goggles

Wear goggles or a face shield to protect the eyes against dust, sparks, chemical splashing, flying objects, and other foreign matter.

Ear Plugs and Muffs

Ear protectors will shield against loud noise created by machines and hammering. Excessive noise may damage the ears permanently and cause hearing loss.

Gloves and Barrier Cream

To prevent harmful substances from entering the bloodstream through the skin and to prevent dermatitis, the hands may be covered with gloves or a barrier cream, which is rubbed into the skin. Different creams are used to protect the skin from materials such as acids and plastic resins. However, gloves are more effective.

Ventilation

The aim of ventilating is to remove the contaminants before they reach the worker. Opening windows is not adequate ventilation, and open windows often create more of a hazard by blowing dirt around the work space.

An exhaust fan is most effective for removing contaminated air because it draws the material *away* from the work area. Placement is crucial to the fan's effectiveness; a fan installed in the wrong place may draw dirty air past the worker. Be certain that a fresh supply of air is available to replace the contaminated air. Do not allow exhausted air to re-enter the room through another window or opening.

A hood similar to those used over household stoves helps collect the contaminant so that it can either be drawn outside through a duct or through a filter which is periodically cleaned or replaced.

General Precautions in the Studio

Many common-sense precautions may be taken in the studio to alleviate some of the hazards involved in jewelry making.

- Wash hands frequently, especially after working with hazardous materials.
- Keep the workshop clean and uncluttered. This will help to prevent spills and tripping over equipment, and it will allow more working space.
- Do not eat, smoke, or store food in the studio. This will help to prevent substances from being injested accidently.
- Keep lids on materials to prevent spilling and evaporation and to prevent powders from getting into the air.
- Do not wear loose clothing or jewelry that may get caught in machines or dipped inadvertently into chemicals. Tie hair back, especially when working with a torch or machine.
- Use a vacuum cleaner or damp mop rather than a broom. This will keep airborne dust at a minimum.
- Keep handy a Class ABC fire extinguisher, which is appropriate for extinguishing wood, paper, cloth, solvent, fuel, and electrical fires. Be sure to become familiar with its use.
- Label all materials clearly.
- Use adequate lighting.
- Keep a first-aid kit handy.

Hazardous Substances

The following are substances frequently encountered by jewelers, with suggested safety precautions.

Asbestos

Asbestos is a silicate mineral that is primarily used for its ability to resist heat and acid. Jewelers use asbestos for lining casting flasks, as a soldering surface, and as a heat shield to protect sections of a piece while soldering. Asbestos is a known carcinogen and should not be used if there is any chance that it will enter the body. A respirator with an asbestos dust cartridge provides some protection. Soft asbestos is particularly dangerous because it can flake during use, particularly if it is old. Powdered asbestos should never be used. Hard asbestos (transite) is less hazardous so long as it is not sawed and is disposed of as soon as there is any evidence of flaking.

There are many substitutes for asbestos that are not only safer but are equally effective. Among them are firebrick (of the alumina rather than silica type), pumice, and charcoal. Various new products on the market, distributed under different brand names (Sod-Block is one), are made specifically to replace asbestos. Heavy leather gloves can often be used instead of asbestos gloves.

Acids

Acids such as nitric, hydrochloric, and sulfuric are extremely strong and must be used with great caution. Acids are used in jewelry making to pickle, etch, and color metals. They can burn the skin and damage the lungs. Sparex, a commercial pickling agent, becomes an acid when mixed with water. Nitric acid fumes are particularly dangerous and may cause death.

Precautions to be taken when using acids:
- Local exhaust ventilation is essential. A respirator with an acid-gas cartridge is also effective.
- Acids should be kept covered at all times.
- Always add the acid to the water.
- Wear protective clothing and goggles.

Benzene

Benzene (benzol) is highly toxic; less toxic solvents should always be substituted. Benzene has a cumulative effect and can cause death. Benzine is a commonly used, relatively safe solvent and should not be confused with benzene. But all organic solvents should be used only with adequate ventilation, and skin contact and accidental ingestion should be avoided.

Cadmium

Cadmium is a hazard that may be encountered when soldering because it is present in some silver solders. The fumes created when this metal is heated are extremely toxic. Cadmium can cause chemical pneumonia. Substitute alloys should be used. When purchasing solder, always ask about the content of the alloy. Adequate ventilation is essential when soldering.

Casting

Casting involves a number of hazards. The high temperatures it requires may produce noxious fumes (see *Metal Fumes* below). Heating the investment may release hazardous materials into the air, so always vent the casting kiln to the outside and work under a canopy-type hood.

Vapors from heated wax used in model making should be avoided and local exhaust ventilation always used. The eyes should be shielded from the infrared radiation from the kiln. Wear special goggles if a great deal of casting is to be done.

Wear an approved dust mask when working with large quantities of investment.

Fluorides

Fluorides are found in some fluxes, and when combined with the fluids in the body, they will produce hydrofluoric acid. This occurs during soldering when the vapors are created. The resulting acid may cause damage to the respiratory tract. Regular exposure to fluorides can cause damage to bones and teeth. All soldering should be done with local exhaust ventilation.

Grinding and Polishing

Grinding and polishing fills the air with small particles that could be hazardous. Organic materials such as wood, shell, and bone may cause allergic reactions. Long-term exposure to dust of stones containing free silica (quartz) can cause silicosis, which leaves the lungs weak and susceptible to respiratory diseases. Some stones such as serpentine and soapstone may contain particles of asbestos. Grinding these materials should be done only while wearing a respirator with a dust filter.

Metal Fumes

Metal fumes are created when metals are heated to high temperatures, as in casting and soldering. The higher the temperature, the greater the possibility of vaporization of the different metals. The fumes from zinc (alloyed in some solders, nickel silver, and brass, as well as other metals), copper, and iron can cause a condition known as *fume fever*. Symptoms occur a few hours after exposure and last for a day or two. They are similar to flu symptoms.

Soft solders (sometimes used in jewelry making) contain lead, which may give off fumes at excessively high temperatures. Lead is also present in some metal alloys, although most alloys sold today do not contain it. Lead is also a cumulative poison.

Fumes from silver, platinum, and tin should also be avoided. Good ventilation is essential, and a respirator with a toxic-fumes filter should be used.

Plastics

Plastics are worked in various ways including grinding, machining, filing, cutting, casting, and heat forming. Skin contact and breathing the vapors and dust can be dangerous. Use adequate ventilation, wear an organic-vapor respirator, and protect skin and eyes whenever working with plastics. Disposable plastic gloves will protect the hands.

Epoxy resin is irritating to the skin and may cause dermatitis. Skin contact should be avoided, especially with the hardener. Fumes created in curing can also be irritating, and the catalyst is a severe eye irritant. Polyesters give off styrene vapors, which can be harmful to the liver, lungs, blood, and nervous systems. Wear a respirator with an organic-vapor cartridge and protective goggles.

Tables

Scale of Cuts for Dixon Grobet Swiss Precision Files

Teeth per inch (upcut)	30	38	51	64	79
Files 10″ and over in length	00	0	1	2	3
Files 4″ to 8″ in length		00	0	1	2
Files 3″ in length			00	0	1
Escapement Files				0	
Needle Files 4″ to 7¾″				0	
Regular Rifflers				0	

Teeth per inch (upcut)	97	117	142	173	213	295
Files 10″ and over in length	4		6			
Files 4″ to 8″ in length	3	4		6		
Files 3″ in length	2	3	4		6	
Escapement Files	2	3	4		6	8
Needle Files 4″ to 7¾″	2	3	4		6	
Regular Rifflers	2	3	4		6	

Courtesy of William Dixon Company.

Swiss	00	0	No. 2
American	Bastard	Second Cut	Smooth Cut

Courtesy of William Dixon Company.

Dixon Scies-Saws Blade Sizes

Size Number	Thickness	Width	Comparative Blade
8/0	.006″	.013″	(Saws finer
7/0	.007	.014	than 4/0
6/0	.007	.014	not illustrated)
5/0	.008	.015	
4/0	.008	.017	
3/0	.010	.019	
2/0	.010	.020	
0	.011	.023	
1	.012	.025	
2	.014	.027	
3	.014	.029	
4	.015	.031	
5	.016	.034	
6	.019	.041	
8	.020	.048	
10	.020	.058	
12	.023	.064	
14	.024	.068	

Courtesy of William Dixon Company

Dixon Silver Solder

Silver (hard) solder is a special silver alloy similar to sterling but having a lower melting point. In addition to soldering silver, it is also used on small joints of copper, brass, nickel silver, and such. Varying flow points make it easy and practical to have multiple solderings on the same piece.

Type	Melting Point °F(°C)	Flow Point °F(°C)	Percentage Composition				Description
			Silver	Copper	Zinc	Other	
Easy Flo 45	1125 (607)	1145 (618)	45	15	16	24 (CAD)	Most popular hard solder for industry
Easy	1145 (618)	1205 (652)	56	22	17	5 (TIN)	Good white color preferred by jewelers
Medium	1275 (691)	1360 (738)	70	20	10	—	Excellent color for extra strong joints
Hard	1365 (741)	1450 (788)	75	22	3	—	For multiple joint work

Courtesy of William Dixon Company.

Dixon Gold Solder

Karat	Melting Point °F	(°C)
8	1435	(780)
10	1410	(766)
12	1420	(771)
14	1360	(738)

Courtesy of William Dixon Company.

Specific Gravity of Metals

To determine the weight of the metal needed to cast a wax model:

1. Weight the wax model (in grams) with the sprues attached.
2. Find the specific gravity of the metal that you are casting.
3. Multiply the weight of the wax by the specific gravity. Your answer will be the weight of the metal needed for the casting (in grams).

Metal	Specific Gravity
Gold	
24K	19.4
18K	15.6
14K	13.4
10K	11.6
Silver	
Fine	10.5
Sterling	10.4
Bronze	9.0
Brass	8.5

Mohs Scale of Hardness

1. Talc
2. Gypsum
3. Calcite
4. Fluorite
5. Apatite
6. Feldspar
7. Quartz
8. Topaz
9. Corundum
10. Diamond

Relative Hardness of Materials According to the Mohs Scale

Soapstone 1 to 1½
Alabaster 2
Ivory 2½
Amber 2½
Serpentine 2½ to 3
Coral 3½
Jet 2½ to 4
Pearl 3 to 4
Howlite 3½
Opal, turquoise 6
Steel 6 to 7
Amethyst, onyx, citrine, tiger eye, agate 7
Emerald 8
Sapphire, ruby 9

Basic Equipment List

General

Adjustable 5″ saw frame
Saw blades #1/0
Bench pin
Bench vise
Steel surface plate
Chasing hammer
Planishing hammer
Large shears
Hand drill
Twist drills
Center punch
Steel rule
Scribe
Chain-nose pliers
Flat-nose pliers
Round-nose pliers
Needle file set
Half-round file, #2 cut
Hand file, #0 cut
Rawhide or wooden mallet
Bezel pusher
Burnisher
Cutting nippers
V board and clamp

Soldering

2 pairs crosslock tweezers
Soldering pick
Tripod with wire mesh
Torch
Transite pad, 12″ × 12″ (30.5 × 30.5 cm), or firebrick
Small brush
Hard solder flux
Pickling solution (Sparex)
Pyrex covered dish or ceramic slow cooker
Copper tongs
Hard, medium, and easy solder
Charcoal block
Brass wire brush
Striker

Polishing

2 hand polishing sticks or polishing machine with two buffs and hood
Emery paper, 240, 320, 400, 600 grit
Crocus cloth
Tripoli compound
Rouge
Goggles
Respirator with dust filter

Casting

Casting wax (sheet, wire, etc.)
Wax carving tools

Alcohol lamp
Denatured alcohol
Wax file
Centrifugal casting machine or
    steam caster
Flasks and sprue bases
Casting tongs
Investment
Borax
Rubber bowl
Spatula
Debubblizer
Heavy leather gloves
Furnace
Poker

ADDITIONAL TOOLS

Ring sizer
Ring mandrel
Bracelet mandrel

Dividers
Graver
Chasing tools
Pitch bowl
Dapping die and punches
Wire and sheet gauge
Raising hammer
Riveting hammer
Anvils
Riffle files
Bezel shears
Hollow scraper
Engraving tool
Hand vise
Mounted tweezers (third hand)
Flexible shaft with accessories for
    polishing, grinding, etc.
Screwplate with taps
Rolling mill
Pin vise, swivel head
Charcoal ring stick

Sources of Supplies

All tools mentioned in this book can be purchased at a jewelry supply store. Some items such as drill bits, emery paper, brass and copper wire, files, and propane torches are commonly stocked by hardware stores. A local hobby or art store may also carry some of the needed items. Local art centers or school art departments might also be able to suggest sources for materials.

Craft Items

AMACO
4717 West 16th Street
Indianapolis, IN 46222
(ceramic supplies)

Grey Owl Indian Craft
   Manufacturing Co.
150-02 Beaver Road
Jamaica, NY 11433
(feathers, beads, mirrors)

Hollywood Fancy Feather
512 South Broadway
Los Angeles, CA 90013
(feathers)

J. I. Morris Company
P.O. Box 70
Southbridge, MA 01550
(small brass nuts and bolts)

Naturalcraft Inc.
2199 Bancroft Way
Berkeley, CA 94704
(feathers, bells, beads)

School Products Co. Inc.
1201 Broadway
New York, NY 10001
(yarn, weaving supplies)

Custom Casting

Billanti Casting Co., Inc.
64 West 48th Street
New York, NY 10036
(will send through the mail)

Design Stamps

Alpha Tool and Die
7 West 45th Street
New York, NY 10036
(signature, logo, and design stamps)

H. A. Evers Company, Inc.
72-C Oxford Street
Providence, RI 02905
(signature, logo, and design stamps)

Display

Abstracta Structures Inc.
101 Park Avenue
New York, NY 10017
(tubular structural display system)

Box Stylist Corporation
235–N Robbins Lane
Syosset, NY 11791
(boxes, jewelry display items)

Gerald Fried Display Co. Inc.
550 Filmore Avenue
Tonawanda, NY 14150
(cases, boxes, jewelry display items)

Gems and Stones

Baskin & Sons, Inc.
732 Union Avenue
Middlesex, NJ 08846

Ernest W. Bessinger
P.O. Box 454
Carnegie, PA 15106

Canadice Manufacturing Co.
Seneca Building, Terrace Level
P.O. Box 9617 Midtown Plaza
Rochester, NY 14604

Frazier's Minerals & Lapidary
1724 University Avenue
Berkeley, CA 94703

Grieger's Inc.
900 South Arroyo Parkway
Pasadena, CA 91109
(lapidary equipment, stones, tools)

Treasure of the Pirates
4840 Rugby Avenue
Bethesda, MD 20014

Wards Natural Science
    Establishment Inc.
P.O. Box 1749
Monterey, CA 93940
(fossils, rocks)

Jewlery Tools, Equipment, and Metal

Allcraft Tool & Supply Co., Inc.
100 Frank Road
Hicksville, NY 11801
(tools, metal, equipment, findings)

Alpha Faceting Supply
Box 2133
Bremerton, WA 98310

Anchor Tool & Supply Co.
231 Main St.
Chatham, NJ 07928

Anozira, Inc.
4002 North Stone
Tucson, AZ 85717

Bourget Brothers
1626 11th Street
Santa Monica, CA 90404

Brookstone Co.
Peterborough, NH 03458
(hard-to-find tools)

Buried Treasure, Inc.
12124 Nebel Street
Rockville, MD 20852

William Dixon Co.
Carlstadt, NJ 07072
(tools, equipment, casting)

Ebersole Lapidary Supply
11417 West Highway 54
Wichita, KS 67209

Paul Gesswein & Co.
255 Hancock Avenue
Bridgeport, CT 06605
(tools, equipment, findings)

T. B. Hagstoz & Son, Inc.
709 Sansom Street
Philadelphia, PA 19106
(metal, tools, equipment, casting)

Hauser and Miller Co.
4011 Forest Park Blvd.
St. Louis, MO 63108
(reticulation silver)

Kerr Manufacturing Co.
Division of Sybron Corp.
P.O. Box 455/28200 Wick Road
Romulus, MI 48174
(casting)

Lapstar, Inc.
4070 S.W. Cedar Hills Blvd.
Beaverton, OR 97005

The Silver Cache
6440 South McClintock
Tempe, AZ 85283

SWEST Inc.
10803 Composite Drive
Dallas, TX 75220
(metal, tools, findings, casting)

Plastics

Cadillac Plastics and Chemical Co.
P.O. Box 810
Detroit, MI 48232
(polyester resin, Plexiglas)

Commercial Plastics and Supply
    Corporation
55 Marine Street
Farmingdale, NY 11735
(Located in many other cities)
(acrylic)

Industrial Plastic Supply Co.
309 Canal Street
New York, NY 10013
(domes, rods, sheets, tubes)

The Plastics Factory
18 East 12th Street
New York, NY 10003
(resins, tools)

Polyproducts Corporation
P.O. Box 42
28510 Hayes Avenue
Roseville, MI 48066
(polyester resins, epoxy enamels,
    pigments)

Wood

Robert M. Albrecht
8635 Yolanda Avenue
Northridge, CA 91324
(veneers, rare and imported woods)

Albert Constantine and Son, Inc.
2050 Eastchester Road
Bronx, NY 10461
(veneers and exotic woods)

Craftsman Wood Service Co.
2727 South Mary Street
Chicago, IL 60608
(veneers, rare and exotic woods)

Bibliography

Casting

Chaote, Sharr. *Creative Casting: Jewelry, Silverware, Sculpture.* New York: Crown, 1966.

Edwards, Keith. *Lost Wax Casting of Jewelry.* Chicago: Henry Regnery, 1975.

Gemstones

Lapidary Journal, 3564 Kettner Blvd., San Diego, Calif. Monthly.

Quick, Lande, and Leiper, Hugh. *Gemcraft: How to Cut and Polish Gemstones.* Radnor, Pa.: Chilton, 1977.

Sinkankas, John. *Gem Cutting: A Lapidary's Manual.* New York: Van Nostrand Reinhold, 1962.

General

American Craft, 22 West 55 Street, New York, 10019. Monthly.

Goldsmiths Journal. The Society of North American Goldsmiths. Art Department, Longwood College, Farmville, VA 23901. Bimonthly.

Ornament, 1221 LaCienega, Los Angeles, CA 90035. Quarterly.

Health Hazards

Art Hazards News. The Center for Occupational Hazards. 5 Beekman Street, New York 10038. Monthly.

Carnow, Bertram. *Health Hazards in the Arts and Crafts.* University of Illinois School of Public Health, 1974.

McCann, Michael. *Artist Beware: The Hazards and Precautions in Working with Art and Craft Materials.* New York: Watson-Guptill, 1979.

————. *Health Hazards Manual for Artists*. New York: Foundation for the Community of Artists, 1975.

Weiss, Linda. "Goldsmithing Health Hazards." *Goldsmiths Journal*, 4, no. 5 (October 1978): 20 A–L.

History and Design

Chatt, Orville. *Design is Where You Find It*. Ames: The Iowa State University Press, 1972.

Gerlach, Martin, ed. *Primitive and Folk Jewelry*. New York: Dover, 1971.

Gregorietti, Guido. *Jewelry Through the Ages*. New York: American Heritage, 1969.

Turner, Ralph. *Contemporary Jewelry*. New York: Van Nostrand Reinhold, 1976.

Willcox, Donald. *New Design in Jewelry*. New York: Van Nostrand Reinhold, 1970.

————. *Body Jewelry: International Perspectives*. Chicago: Henry Regnery, 1973.

Marketing

Contemporary Crafts Market Place, American Crafts Council. New York: R.R. Bowker, 1977.

The Crafts Report: The Newsmonthly of Marketing, Management and Money for Crafts Professionals, 700 Orange Street, P.O. Box 1992, Wilmington, DE 19899. Monthly.

Plastics

Hollander, Harry. *Plastics for Jewelry*. New York: Watson-Guptill, 1974.

Newman, Jay Hartley, and Newman, Lee Scott. *Plastics for the Craftsman*. New York: Crown, 1972.

Newman, Thelma. *Plastics as an Art Form*. Radnor, Pa.: Chilton, 1964.

Technique

Chamberlain, Marcia. *Metal Jewelry Techniques*. New York: Watson-Guptill, 1976.

Choate, Sharr. *Creative Gold and Silversmithing: Jewelry, Decorative Metalcraft*. New York: Crown, 1970.

Coyne, John, ed. *The Penland School of Crafts Book of Jewelry Making*. New York: Bobbs-Merrill, 1975.

DiPasquale, Dominic. *Jewelry Making: An Illustrated Guide to Technique*. Englewood Cliffs, N.J.: Prentice-Hall, 1975.

Fisch, Arline. *Textile Techniques in Metal for Jewelers, Sculptors, and Textile Artists*. New York: Van Nostrand Reinhold, 1975.

Gentille, Thomas. *Step-by-Step Jewelry: A Complete Introduction to the Craft of Jewelry*. New York: Golden Press, 1968.

Gonsalves, Alyson Smith, ed. *Jewelry You Can Make*. Menlo Park, Calif.: Lane Publishing, 1975.

Hardy, R. Allen. *The Jewelry Engraver's Manual*, rev. ed. New York: Van Nostrand Reinhold, 1976.

————, and Bowman, John. *Jewelry Repair Manual*. New York: Van Nostrand Reinhold, 1976.

Morton, Philip. *Contemporary Jewelry: A Studio Handbook*, rev. ed. New York: Holt, Rinehart and Winston, 1976.

O'Connor, Harold. *New Directions in Goldsmithing*. Crested Butte, Colo.: Donconor Books, 1976.

————. *Procedures and Formulas for Metal Craftsmen*. Crested Butte, Colo.: Donconor Books, 1976.

Seppa, Heikki. *Form Emphasis for Metalsmiths*. Kent, Ohio: The Kent State University Press, 1978.

Sommer, Elyse. *Contemporary Costume Jewelry: A Multimedia Approach*. New York: Crown, 1974.

Steen, Carol. "The Masonite Die: An Examination of the One Plane Masonite Die In Combination With Secondary Forms." M.F.A. thesis, Cranbrook Academy of Art, 1971.

von Neumann, Robert. The Design and Creation of Jewelry, rev. ed. Radnor, Pa.: Chilton, 1972.

Index

Page numbers in **bold** refer to illustrations.